Wok

Bath · New York · Singapore · Hong Kong · Cologne · Delhi · Melbourne

This edition published by Parragon in 2009

Parragon Publishing
Queen Street House
4 Queen Street
Bath BA1 1HE, UK

ISBN: 978-1-4075-8034-0

Printed in China

Notes for the Reader
This book uses imperial, metric, and U.S. cup measurements. Follow the same units of measurement throughout; do not mix imperial and metric. All spoon measurements are level: teaspoons are assumed to be 5 ml, and tablespoons are assumed to be 15 ml. Unless otherwise stated, milk is assumed to be whole, eggs and individual vegetables, such as potatoes, are medium, and pepper is freshly ground black pepper.

The times given are an approximate guide only. Preparation times differ according to the techniques used by different people and the cooking times may also vary from those given as a result of the type of oven used. Optional ingredients, variations, or serving suggestions have not been included in the calculations.

Recipes using raw or very lightly cooked eggs should be avoided by infants, the elderly, pregnant women, convalescents, and anyone with a chronic condition. Pregnant and breastfeeding women are advised to avoid eating peanuts and peanut products. People with nut allergies should be aware that some of the prepared ingredients used in the recipes in this book may contain nuts. Always check the packaging before use.

Picture acknowledgements
The publisher would like to thank Hein van den Heuvel/Zefa/Corbis for permission to reproduce copyright material for the front cover

Wok

introduction

As you will soon see when you start cooking recipes from this book, buying a good wok is one of the best investments in kitchen equipment that you will ever make. This incredibly versatile pan can be used for soups, deep-frying, steaming, and, most importantly, for stir-frying, the favorite cooking method of the people of Southeast and East Asia.

Wok cooking is ideal for anyone who is always on the go, because the dishes are nutritious, very quick and easy to prepare and cook, and absolutely delicious. Cooked rapidly over a high heat, vegetables retain their crisp texture and vibrant color, so that

the visual appeal of a stir-fried dish matches its taste, and meat, poultry, fish, bean curd, or nuts add protein. Wonderful sauces, made in advance and then stirred in to heat through before serving, add a finishing touch.

A traditional wok is made of steel, and when you get it home it will need a little preparation before use, known as "seasoning." First of all, scrub off the protective oiled coating in warm, soapy water, rinse well, and let half dry. Next, let the damp wok stand on a hob over low heat until it is completely dry. Drizzle in a little oil and wipe it round the inside with paper towels. Continue heating until the oil smokes and burns off, then repeat with another coating of oil. The wok will darken in color and should never need scrubbing again, just wiping carefully.

You can prepare for wok and stir-fry cooking by buying in a few store-cupboard ingredients. Items such as rice and a variety of noodles, peanut, sesame, and vegetable oils, coconut milk, soy

sauce, canned water chestnuts and straw mushrooms, fish sauce, curry pastes, spices, and cornstarch will get you started and all you'll need are the fresh ingredients to enable you to whip up a feast in moments.

Take to the wok and have fun!

soups &
appetizers

You might never have thought of making soup in a wok, but the people of Thailand and China do it all the time! Start with the classic chicken noodle soup and you will soon discover the joys of the wonderful flavors and textures that go into soups from this part of the world. Coconut milk is sometimes used, giving a rich, creamy result, but often the soup is a simple broth of vegetables, usually with a little meat, poultry, or fish added.

If you are a lover of Chinese and Thai food, you'll be pleased to find that some of your favorite appetizers—the ones that you are often tempted to buy in packages because they look complicated—are actually very quick and easy to make. Those delicious, crispy, little parcels that hold various tasty fillings—spring rolls, wontons, and dumplings—take just a few minutes to construct and an additional couple of minutes to cook, and once you've tasted them fresh from the wok, well drained on paper towels, you'll never go back to buying them. Try making delicious Japanese tempura, too—vegetables cooked in a coating of crisp, light batter. When deep-frying, remember that the fat needs to stay really hot to give the best result, so cook in small batches and keep each batch warm as you cook the next.

chicken noodle soup

ingredients

SERVES 4–6

1 sheet dried egg noodles
from a 9 oz/250 g package
1 tbsp corn oil
4 skinless, boneless chicken
thighs, diced
1 bunch of scallions, sliced
2 garlic cloves, chopped
3/4-inch/2-cm piece fresh
gingerroot, finely chopped
1 1/2 pints/850 ml/3 3/4 cups
chicken stock
6 fl oz/175 ml/generous
3/4 cup coconut milk
3 tsp Thai red curry paste
3 tbsp peanut butter
2 tbsp light soy sauce
salt and pepper
1 small red bell pepper,
seeded and chopped
2 oz/55 g/1/2 cup frozen peas

method

1 Place the noodles in a shallow heatproof dish and let soak in boiling water according to the package directions.

2 Meanwhile, heat the oil in a preheated wok. Add the chicken and stir-fry for 5 minutes, or until lightly browned. Add the white part of the scallions, the garlic, and gingerroot and stir-fry for 2 minutes.

3 Add the stock, coconut milk, curry paste, peanut butter, and soy sauce. Season to taste with salt and pepper. Bring to a boil, stirring constantly, then simmer for 8 minutes, stirring occasionally. Add the bell pepper, peas, and green scallion tops and cook for an additional 2 minutes.

4 Drain the noodles, then add them to the wok and heat through. Spoon into warmed serving bowls and serve immediately.

duck with scallion soup

ingredients

SERVES 4

2 duck breasts, skin on

2 tbsp Thai red curry paste

2 tbsp vegetable or peanut oil

bunch of scallions, chopped

2 garlic cloves, crushed

2-inch piece fresh
   gingerroot, grated

2 carrots, sliced thinly

1 red bell pepper, seeded and
   cut into strips

1³/₄ pints/1 liter/4 cups
   chicken stock

2 tbsp sweet chili sauce

3–4 tbsp Thai soy sauce

14 oz/400 g canned straw
   mushrooms, drained

method

1 Slash the skin of the duck 3 or 4 times with a sharp knife and rub in the curry paste. Cook the duck breasts, skin-side down, in a wok over high heat for 2–3 minutes. Turn over, reduce the heat, and cook for an additional 3–4 minutes, until cooked through. Lift out and slice thickly. Set aside and keep warm.

2 Meanwhile, heat the oil in a wok and stir-fry half the scallions, the garlic, gingerroot, carrots, and the red bell pepper for 2–3 minutes. Pour in the stock and add the chili sauce, soy sauce, and mushrooms. Bring to a boil, reduce the heat, and let simmer for 4–5 minutes.

3 Ladle the soup into warmed bowls, top with the duck slices, and garnish with the remaining scallions. Serve immediately.

thai-style seafood soup

ingredients

SERVES 4

2 1/4 pints/1.25 liters/5 cups
    fish stock
1 lemongrass stem, split
    lengthwise
pared rind of 1/2 lime or
    1 fresh kaffir lime leaf
1-inch/2.5-cm piece fresh
    gingerroot, sliced
1/4 tsp chili paste, or to taste
4–6 scallions
7 oz/200 g large or medium
    raw shrimp, shelled
salt
9 oz/250 g scallops (16–20)
2 tbsp cilantro leaves
finely chopped red bell
    pepper or fresh red chile
    rings, to garnish

method

1 Place the stock in a wok with the lemongrass, lime rind, gingerroot, and chili paste. Bring just to a boil, then reduce the heat and simmer, covered, for 10–15 minutes.

2 Cut the scallions in half lengthwise, then slice crosswise very thinly. Cut the shrimp almost in half lengthwise, keeping the tails intact. Devein if necessary.

3 Pour the stock through a strainer, then return to the wok and bring to a simmer, with bubbles rising at the edges and the surface trembling. Add the scallions and cook for 2–3 minutes. Taste and season with salt, if needed. Stir in a little more chili paste if wished.

4 Add the scallops and shrimp and poach for 1 minute, or until they turn opaque and the shrimp curl.

5 Drop in the cilantro leaves, then ladle the soup into warmed serving bowls, dividing the shellfish evenly, and garnish with bell pepper or chili rings.

corn & crab soup

ingredients

SERVES 4

2 tbsp vegetable or peanut oil

4 garlic cloves, chopped finely

5 shallots, chopped finely

2 lemongrass stalks, chopped finely

1-inch piece fresh gingerroot, chopped finely

$1^3/_4$ pints/1 liter/4 cups chicken stock

14 oz/400 g canned coconut milk

6 oz/175 g/scant $1^1/_2$ cups frozen corn kernels

12 oz/350 g canned crabmeat, drained and shredded

2 tbsp fish sauce

juice of 1 lime

1 tsp jaggery or soft light brown sugar

bunch of fresh cilantro, chopped, to garnish

method

1 Heat the oil in a wok and sauté the garlic, shallots, lemongrass, and gingerroot over low heat, stirring occasionally, for 2–3 minutes, or until softened.

2 Add the stock and coconut milk and bring to a boil. Add the corn, reduce the heat, and let simmer gently for 3–4 minutes.

3 Add the crabmeat, fish sauce, lime juice, and sugar, and let simmer gently for 1 minute.

4 Ladle into warmed bowls, garnish with the chopped cilantro, and serve immediately.

spicy thai soup with shrimp

ingredients

SERVES 4

2 tbsp tamarind paste

4 fresh red Thai chilies,
    very finely chopped

2 garlic cloves, crushed

1-inch/2.5-cm piece fresh
    galangal, very finely
    chopped

4 tbsp Thai fish sauce

2 tbsp palm sugar or
    superfine sugar

8 fresh kaffir lime leaves,
    coarsely torn

$1^3/_4$ pints/1 liter/4 cups
    fish stock

4 oz/125 g/1 cup very thinly
    sliced carrots

6 oz/175 g/2 cups diced
    sweet potato

$3^1/_2$ oz/100 g baby corn cobs,
    halved

3 tbsp cilantro, coarsely
    chopped

$3^1/_2$ oz/100 g cherry
    tomatoes, halved

8 oz/225 g cooked fantail
    shrimp

method

1 Place the tamarind paste, chilies, garlic, galangal, fish sauce, sugar, lime leaves, and stock in a large, preheated wok. Bring to a boil, stirring constantly.

2 Reduce the heat and add the carrots, sweet potato, and baby corn cobs to the mixture in the wok.

3 Let the soup simmer for 10 minutes, or until the vegetables are just tender.

4 Stir the cilantro, cherry tomatoes, and shrimp into the soup and heat through for 5 minutes.

5 Transfer the soup to warmed serving bowls and serve hot.

vegetable & noodle soup

ingredients

SERVES 4

2 tbsp vegetable or peanut oil

1 onion, sliced

2 garlic cloves, chopped finely

1 large carrot, cut into thin
   sticks

1 zucchini, cut into thin sticks

4 oz/115 g broccoli, cut into
   florets

$1^3/_4$ pints/1 liter/4 cups
   vegetable stock

14 fl oz/400 ml/$1^3/_4$ cups
   coconut milk

3–4 tbsp Thai soy sauce

2 tbsp Thai red curry paste

2 oz/55 g wide rice noodles

4 oz/115 g/$^3/_4$ cup mung or
   soy bean sprouts

4 tbsp chopped fresh cilantro

method

1 Heat the oil in a wok and stir-fry the onion and garlic for 2–3 minutes.

2 Add the carrot, zucchini, and broccoli and stir-fry for 3–4 minutes, until just tender.

3 Pour in the stock and coconut milk and bring to a boil. Add the soy sauce, curry paste, and noodles, and let simmer for 2–3 minutes, until the noodles have swelled.

4 Stir in the bean sprouts and cilantro and serve immediately.

mushroom & noodle soup

ingredients

SERVES 4

$^1/_2$ cucumber

2 tbsp vegetable oil

2 scallions, finely chopped

1 garlic clove, cut into thin
   strips

$4^1/_2$ oz/125 g/2 cups flat or
   open-cap mushrooms,
   thinly sliced

1 pint/600 ml/$2^1/_2$ cups water

1 oz/25 g Chinese rice
   noodles

$^3/_4$ tsp salt

1 tbsp soy sauce

method

1 Halve the cucumber lengthwise. Scoop out the seeds using a teaspoon, then slice the flesh thinly.

2 Heat the oil in a large preheated wok. Add the scallions and garlic and stir-fry for 30 seconds. Add the mushrooms and stir-fry for 2–3 minutes.

3 Stir in the water. Break the noodles into short lengths and add to the soup. Bring to a boil, stirring.

4 Add the cucumber slices, salt, and soy sauce, and let simmer for 2–3 minutes.

5 Ladle the soup into warmed bowls, distributing the noodles and vegetables evenly.

rice noodles with bean curd soup

ingredients

SERVES 4

7 oz/200 g firm bean curd,
  drained
vegetable or peanut oil,
  for deep-frying
$1^3/_4$ pints/1 liter/4 cups
  vegetable stock
5 scallions, halved
1 yellow bell pepper, seeded
  and sliced
2 celery stalks, sliced
1 small onion, sliced thinly
4 kaffir lime leaves
2 tbsp Thai soy sauce
1 tbsp Thai green curry paste
6 oz/175 g wide rice noodles,
  soaked and drained
chopped fresh cilantro,
  to garnish

method

1 Using a sharp knife, cut the bean curd into even cubes. Pour the oil into a wok to a depth of about 2 inches and heat. Deep-fry the bean curd, in batches, until browned all over. Remove with a slotted spoon, drain on paper towels, and set aside.

2 Pour the stock into the clean wok and bring to a boil. Add the scallions, yellow bell pepper, celery, onion, lime leaves, soy sauce, and curry paste, and let simmer for 4–5 minutes. Add the noodles and the bean curd and let simmer for 2–3 minutes.

3 Ladle into warmed bowls and serve hot, topped with chopped cilantro.

kara-age chicken

ingredients

SERVES 4

6 skinless, boneless
chicken thighs, about
3^1/$_2$ oz/100 g each

4 tbsp shoyu (Japanese
soy sauce)

4 tbsp mirin

2 tsp finely grated fresh
gingerroot

2 garlic cloves, crushed

oil, for deep-frying

2^1/$_2$ oz/70 g/^{1}/$_2$ cup potato
starch or cornstarch

pinch of salt

lemon wedges, to serve

method

1 Cut the chicken into large cubes and put in a bowl. Add the soy sauce, mirin, gingerroot, and garlic and turn the chicken to coat well. Cover with plastic wrap and let marinate in a cool place for 20 minutes.

2 Preheat a wok, then fill one-third full with oil, or use a deep-fryer. Heat the oil to 350–375°F/180–190°C, or until a cube of bread browns in 30 seconds.

3 Meanwhile, mix the potato starch with the salt in a bowl. Lift the chicken out of the marinade and shake off any excess. Drop it into the potato starch and coat well, then shake off any excess.

4 Add the chicken to the oil, in batches, and cook for 6 minutes, or until crisp and brown. Remove, drain on paper towels, and keep hot while you cook the remaining chicken.

5 Serve with lemon wedges.

beef stir-fry

ingredients

SERVES 4

2 tbsp vegetable or peanut oil

2 medium red onions, sliced
    thinly

2 garlic cloves, chopped

1-inch piece ginger, cut into
    thin sticks

2 x 4-oz/115-g beef fillets,
    sliced thinly

1 green bell pepper, seeded
    and sliced

5^1/$_2$ oz/150 g canned
    bamboo shoots

4 oz/115 g/^{3}/$_4$ cup
    bean sprouts

2 tbsp Thai magic paste
    (see below)

1 tbsp Thai red curry paste

handful of fresh cilantro,
    chopped

few sprigs Thai basil

boiled rice, to serve

thai magic paste

whole bulb of garlic, peeled

bunch of fresh cilantro
    leaves and roots,
    coarsely chopped

2 oz/55 g white peppercorns

method

1 To make the Thai magic paste, pulse all the ingredients briefly in a blender or food processor to form a thick paste, or pound with a pestle until well mixed. Store in the refrigerator for 3–4 days or freeze in small amounts.

2 Heat the oil in a wok and stir-fry the onions, garlic, and gingerroot for 1 minute.

3 Add the beef strips and stir-fry over high heat until browned all over.

4 Add the vegetables and the magic and curry pastes and cook for 2–3 minutes until blended and cooked.

5 Stir in the cilantro and basil and serve immediately with rice.

crispy pork dumplings

ingredients

SERVES 4

12 oz/350 g/1^1/$_2$ cups
    ground pork
2 tbsp finely chopped fresh
    cilantro
1 garlic clove, crushed
1 fresh green chile, seeded
    and chopped
3 tbsp cornstarch
1 egg white
^{1}/$_2$ tsp salt
16 wonton skins
1 tbsp water
vegetable or peanut oil,
    for cooking
chili sauce, to serve

method

1 Put the pork in a bowl and beat in the cilantro, garlic, chile, 1 tablespoon of the cornstarch, the egg white, and salt. Beat together to a thick, smooth texture. With damp hands shape into 16 equal portions and roll into balls.

2 Put a pork ball in the center of each wonton skin. Make a paste by mixing the remaining cornstarch with 1 tablespoon of water. Brush the edges of the skins with the cornstarch paste and gather them up around the filling to make half into small, sacklike packages, and the rest into triangular shapes.

3 Arrange the dumplings in a single layer (in batches if need be) in the top of a steamer and cook over boiling water for 10–15 minutes, until the meat is cooked through.

4 Heat the oil in a wok and carefully drop the packages into it. Deep-fry for 2–3 minutes, until golden brown and crisp. Drain on paper towels.

5 Serve hot with chili sauce.

soft-wrapped pork & shrimp rolls

ingredients

MAKES 20 PIECES

4 oz/115 g firm bean curd

3 tbsp vegetable or peanut oil

1 tsp finely chopped garlic

2 oz/55 g lean pork, shredded

4 oz/115 g raw shrimp,
    peeled and deveined

$^1/_2$ small carrot, cut into short
    thin sticks

2 oz/55 g/$^1/_2$ cup fresh or
    canned bamboo shoots,
    rinsed and shredded (if
    using fresh shoots, boil in
    water first for 30 minutes)

4 oz/115 g/1 cup very finely
    sliced cabbage

2 oz/55 g/$^1/_2$ cup snow peas,
    julienned

1-egg omelet, shredded

1 tsp salt

1 tsp light soy sauce

1 tsp Shaoxing rice wine

pinch of white pepper

20 soft spring roll skins

chili bean sauce, to serve

method

1 Slice the bean curd into thin slices horizontally and cook in 1 tablespoon of the oil until it turns golden brown. Cut into thin strips and set aside.

2 In a preheated wok, heat the remaining oil and stir-fry the garlic until fragrant. Add the pork and stir for about 1 minute, then add the shrimp and stir for an additional minute.

3 One by one, stirring well after each addition, add the carrot, bamboo shoots, cabbage, snow peas, bean curd, and, finally, the shredded omelet.

4 Season with the salt, light soy sauce, Shaoxing rice wine, and pepper. Stir for an additional minute, then turn out into a serving dish.

5 To assemble each roll, smear a skin with a little chili bean sauce and place a heaped teaspoon of the filling toward the bottom of the circle. Roll up the bottom edge to secure the filling, turn in the sides, and continue to roll up gently.

spring rolls

ingredients

MAKES 20–25 PIECES

6 dried Chinese mushrooms,
   soaked in warm water
   for 20 minutes
1 tbsp vegetable or peanut oil
8 oz/225 g/2 cups
   ground pork
1 tsp dark soy sauce
$3^1/_2$ oz/110 g/1 cup fresh or
   canned bamboo shoots,
   rinsed and julienned (if
   using fresh shoots, boil in
   water first for 30 minutes)
pinch of salt
$3^1/_2$ oz/100 g raw shrimp,
   peeled, deveined, and
   chopped
8 oz/225 g/generous
   $1^1/_2$ cups bean sprouts,
   trimmed and coarsely
   chopped
1 tbsp finely chopped
   scallions
25 spring roll skins
1 egg white, lightly beaten
vegetable or peanut oil,
   for deep-frying

method

1 Squeeze out any excess water from the mushrooms and finely slice, discarding any tough stems.

2 In a preheated wok, heat the tablespoon of oil and stir-fry the pork until it changes color. Add the dark soy sauce, bamboo shoots, mushrooms, and a little salt. Stir over high heat for 3 minutes.

3 Add the shrimp and cook for 2 minutes, then add the bean sprouts and cook for an additional minute. Remove from the heat and stir in the scallion. Let cool.

4 Place a tablespoon of the mixture toward the bottom of a skin. Roll once to secure the filling, then fold in the sides to create a 4-inch/10-cm piece and continue to roll up. Seal with egg white.

5 Heat enough oil for deep-frying in a wok or deep-fat fryer until it reaches 180–190°C/350–375°F, or until a cube of bread browns in 30 seconds. Without overcrowding the wok, fry the rolls for about 5 minutes until golden brown and crispy.

crispy wrapped shrimp

ingredients

SERVES 4

16 large, unpeeled cooked
   shrimp
juice of 1 lime
4 tbsp chili sauce
16 wonton skins
vegetable or peanut oil,
   for deep-frying
plum sauce, to serve

method

1 Remove the heads and shell the shrimp, but leave the tails intact. Place them in a nonmetallic bowl, add the lime juice, and toss lightly to coat. Set aside in a cool place for 30 minutes.

2 Spread a little chili sauce over a wonton skin. Place a shrimp diagonally across it, leaving the tail protruding. Fold the bottom corner of the skin over the shrimp, fold the next corner up over the head, and then roll the shrimp up in the skin so that the body is encased, but the tail is exposed. Repeat with the remaining skins, chili sauce, and shrimp.

3 Heat the oil in a wok and deep-fry the shrimp, in batches, until crisp and browned. Serve hot with plum sauce for dipping.

shrimp toasts

ingredients

MAKES 16 PIECES

3$^{1}/_{2}$ oz/100 g raw shrimp,
   peeled, and deveined

2 egg whites

2 tbsp cornstarch

$^{1}/_{2}$ tsp sugar

pinch of salt

2 tbsp finely chopped cilantro
   leaves

2 slices day-old white bread

vegetable or peanut oil, for
   deep-frying

method

1 Pound the shrimp to a pulp in a pestle and mortar or with the base of a cleaver.

2 Mix the shrimp with one of the egg whites and 1 tablespoon of the cornstarch. Add the sugar and salt and stir in the chopped cilantro. Mix the remaining egg white with the remaining cornstarch.

3 Remove the crusts from the bread and cut each slice into 8 triangles. Brush the top of each piece with the egg white and cornstarch mixture, then add 1 teaspoon of the shrimp mixture. Smooth the top.

4 Heat enough oil for deep-frying in a wok until it reaches 350–375°F/180–190°C, or until a cube of bread browns in 30 seconds. Without overcrowding the wok, cook the toasts shrimp-side up for about 2 minutes. Turn and cook for an additional 2 minutes, or until beginning to turn golden brown.

5 Drain and serve warm.

crisp sesame shrimp

ingredients

SERVES 4

4 oz/115 g/^{3}/$_4$ cup
self-rising flour

3 tbsp sesame seeds, toasted
or dry-fried

1 tsp Thai red curry paste

1 tbsp fish sauce

5 fl oz/150 ml/^{2}/$_3$ cup water

vegetable or peanut oil, for
deep-frying

20 large, uncooked shrimp,
shelled with tails intact

chili sauce, for dipping

method

1 Combine the flour and sesame seeds in a bowl. Stir the curry paste, fish sauce, and water together in a pitcher until mixed. Gradually pour the liquid into the flour, stirring constantly, to make a thick batter.

2 Heat the oil for deep-frying in a wok. Holding the shrimp by their tails, dip them into the batter, one at a time, then carefully drop into the hot oil. Cook for 2–3 minutes, until crisp and brown. Drain on paper towels.

3 Serve immediately with chili sauce.

crab parcels

ingredients

SERVES 4

12 oz/350 g canned white
   crabmeat, drained
1 fresh red chile, seeded
   and chopped
4 scallions, sliced finely
1 tbsp Thai red curry paste
juice of $\frac{1}{2}$ lime
$\frac{1}{2}$ tsp salt
20 wonton skins
oil for cooking

dip

2 oz/50 g/generous $\frac{1}{4}$ cup
   superfine sugar
2 tbsp water
2 tbsp rice wine vinegar
3 pieces preserved ginger,
   sliced
1 tbsp ginger syrup from the jar

method

1 Put the crabmeat into a bowl and add the chile, scallions, and curry paste. Stir together with the lime juice and salt.

2 Put the skins in a pile and put 1 portion of the crabmeat in the center of the top skin. Brush the edges with a little water and roll up the edges to make a small cigar-shaped package. Continue to make packages with the skins—you need at least 20.

3 Heat the oil in a wok and cook the packages, a few at a time, until golden brown. Drain on paper towels.

4 Put all the ingredients for the dip in a small pan and heat gently until the sugar has melted. Serve warm with the crab packages.

vegetarian spring rolls

ingredients

MAKES 18–20 PIECES

6 dried Chinese mushrooms,
    soaked in warm water for
    20 minutes

2 oz/55 g beanthread
    noodles, soaked in
    warm water for 20 minutes

2 tbsp vegetable or peanut oil

1 tbsp finely chopped fresh
    gingerroot

$3^{1}/_{2}$ oz/100 g/generous
    $^{2}/_{3}$ cup carrot, julienned

$3^{1}/_{2}$ oz/100 g/scant 1 cup
    finely shredded cabbage

1 tbsp finely sliced scallion

1 tbsp light soy sauce

3 oz/85 g soft bean curd,
    cut into small cubes

$^{1}/_{2}$ tsp salt

pinch of white pepper

pinch of sugar

20 spring roll skins

1 egg white, lightly beaten

vegetable or peanut oil, for
    deep-frying

soy sauce, to serve

method

1 Squeeze out any excess water from the mushrooms and finely chop, discarding any tough stems. Drain the beanthread noodles and coarsely chop.

2 In a preheated wok, heat the oil, then toss in the ginger and cook until fragrant. Add the mushrooms and stir for about 2 minutes. Add the carrot, cabbage, and scallion and stir-fry for 1 minute. Add the beanthread noodles and light soy sauce and stir-fry for 1 minute. Add the bean curd and cook for an additional minute. Season with the salt, pepper, and sugar and mix well. Continue cooking for 1–2 minutes, or until the carrot is soft. Remove from the heat and let cool.

3 Place a scant tablespoon of the mixture toward the bottom of a skin. Roll once to secure the filling, then fold in the sides to create a 4-inch/10-cm piece and continue to roll up. Seal with egg white.

4 Heat enough oil for deep-frying in a wok or deep-fat fryer until it reaches 350–375°F/ 180–190°C, or until a cube of bread browns in 30 seconds. Without overcrowding the wok, cook the rolls for about 5 minutes, or until golden brown and crispy.

5 Serve with a good soy sauce for dipping.

vegetable packages

ingredients

SERVES 4

2 tbsp vegetable or peanut oil

8 oz/225 g potatoes, diced
    and boiled for 5 minutes

2 garlic cloves, crushed

1 onion, chopped

2 tbsp Thai green curry paste

2 oz/55 g/scant $1/2$ cup frozen
    peas, thawed

juice of 1 lime

$1/2$ tsp salt

16 x 4-inch square
    egg roll skins

1 egg, beaten

vegetable or peanut oil, for
    deep-frying

sweet chili sauce or Thai soy
    sauce, to serve

method

1 Heat the oil in a wok and stir-fry the potatoes, garlic, onion, and curry paste until lightly browned. Stir in the peas, lime juice, and salt, and stir-fry for 1–2 minutes. Remove from the heat.

2 Brush 1 egg roll skin with egg. Put a small spoonful of the potato mixture in the center and fold up the edges to enclose the filling and make a purse-shaped package. Press the skin tightly together to seal the package. Repeat with the remaining skins and filling to make 16 small packages.

3 Heat the oil for deep-frying in a wok. Add the vegetable packages, in batches, and deep-fry for 3–4 minutes, until golden brown. Drain on paper towels and keep warm while you cook the remaining packages.

4 Serve hot with a bowl of chili sauce or soy sauce for dipping.

wontons

ingredients

SERVES 4

filling

2 tbsp vegetable or peanut oil

6 scallions, chopped

4$^{1}/_{2}$ oz/125 g mushrooms,
    chopped

2 oz/55 g fine green beans,
    chopped

2 oz/55 g corn kernels,
    drained if canned

1 egg, beaten

3 tbsp Thai soy sauce

1 tbsp jaggery or soft light
    brown sugar

$^{1}/_{2}$ tsp salt

wontons

24 wonton skins

1 egg, beaten

vegetable or peanut oil,
    for deep-frying

plum or chili sauce, to serve

method

1 To make the filling, heat the oil in a preheated wok and stir-fry the scallions, mushrooms, and beans for 1–2 minutes, until softened. Add the corn, stir well to mix, and then push the vegetables to the side.

2 Pour in the egg. Stir until lightly set before incorporating the vegetables and adding the soy sauce, sugar, and salt. Remove the wok from the heat.

3 Place the wonton skins in a pile on a counter. Put a teaspoonful of the filling in the center of the top skin. Brush the edges with beaten egg and fold in half diagonally to make a small triangular package. Repeat with the remaining skins and filling.

4 Heat the oil for deep-frying in a wok. Add the packages, in batches, and deep-fry for 3–4 minutes, until golden brown. Remove from the wok with a slotted spoon and drain on paper towels. Keep warm while you cook the remaining wontons.

5 Serve hot with plum or chili sauce.

crispy seaweed

ingredients

SERVES 4

2 lb 4 oz/1 kg bok choy

1$\frac{1}{2}$ pints/850 ml/about
    3$\frac{1}{2}$ cups peanut oil

1 tsp salt

1 tbsp superfine sugar

3 oz/85 g/generous $\frac{3}{8}$ cup
    toasted pine nuts

method

1 Rinse the bok choy leaves under cold running water, then pat dry thoroughly with paper towels.

2 Discarding any tough outer leaves, roll each bok choy leaf up, then slice thinly so that the leaves are finely shredded. Alternatively, use a food processor to shred the bok choy.

3 Heat the peanut oil in a large preheated wok. Carefully add the shredded bok choy and cook for 30 seconds, or until it shrivels up and becomes crispy. (You will probably need to do this in several batches.) Remove from the wok with a strainer and drain on paper towels.

4 Transfer to a large bowl, toss with the salt, sugar, and toasted pine nuts, and serve.

tempura

ingredients

SERVES 4

5¹/₂ oz/150 g package
   tempura mix
4 shiitake mushrooms
4 fresh asparagus spears
4 slices sweet potato
1 red bell pepper, seeded and
   cut into strips
4 onion slices, cut widthwise
   into rings
oil, for deep-frying

dipping sauce

2 tsp mirin
1 tbsp shoyu (Japanese
   soy sauce)
pinch of dashi granules,
   dissolved in 2 tbsp
   boiling water

method

1 To make the dipping sauce, mix the ingredients together in a small dipping dish.

2 Mix the tempura with water according to the package instructions. Don't try to make the batter smooth—it should be a little lumpy. Drop the vegetables into the batter.

3 Preheat a wok, then fill two-thirds full with oil, or use a deep-fryer. Heat the oil to 350–375°F/180–190°C, or until a cube of bread browns in 30 seconds.

4 Lift 2–3 pieces of tempura out of the batter, add to the oil, and cook for 2–3 minutes, or until the batter is a light golden color. Remove, drain on paper towels, and keep hot while you cook the remaining tempura pieces.

5 Serve with the dipping sauce.

meat &
poultry

Stir-frying is a fast and very efficient way to cook meat and poultry, because the meat is cut into thin strips or small cubes, needing only minutes to cook through. Check your recipe carefully, though, because some dishes require the meat to stand in a marinade for some hours before cooking! Spicy beef with potato is an excellent example—the meat bathes overnight in a paste of soy and fish sauces, herbs, garlic, and peppercorns, but the following day you will need less than 30 minutes to produce a one-pot (or, in this case, one-wok!) meal of tender beef, potatoes, and spinach.

The Thai people often use their woks for cooking curries. Thai curry paste comes in several varieties, including red, green, and yellow, which are readily available in jars. Make sure you use the right color for the recipe, because there is a difference—green is very hot, red is a little less fiery, and yellow is the mildest. Chinese marinades and sauces are lighter and more delicate in flavor, often with a sweet-and-sour taste contrast, while thicker sauces tend to be based on beans.

If you don't yet own a wok, you can use a deep, heavy-bottom pan instead, but the point of the wok is that the shape ensures an even distribution of heat, reducing the cooking time and ensuring that the nutritional value of the ingredients is retained.

mussaman curry

ingredients

SERVES 4

1 tbsp vegetable or peanut oil

1 lb/450 g beef top round,
cut into cubes

2 tbsp Mussaman curry paste

2 large onions, cut into
wedges

2 large potatoes, cut into
chunks

14 fl oz/400 ml/1³/₄ cups
coconut milk

5 fl oz/150 ml/²/₃ cup water

2 cardamom pods

2 tbsp tamarind paste

2 tsp jaggery or soft light
brown sugar

2³/₄ oz/75 g/²/₃ cup unsalted
peanuts, toasted or
dry-fried

1 fresh red chile, sliced thinly

boiled rice, to serve

method

1 Heat the oil in a wok and cook the meat, in batches, until browned all over. Remove with a slotted spoon and set aside.

2 Add the curry paste to the wok and stir-fry for 1–2 minutes. Add the onions and potatoes and stir–fry for 4–5 minutes, until golden brown. Remove with a slotted spoon and set aside.

3 Pour the coconut milk into the wok with the measured water and bring to a boil. Reduce the heat and let simmer for 8–10 minutes.

4 Return the meat and cooked vegetables to the wok. Add the cardamom, tamarind paste, and sugar, and let simmer for 15–20 minutes, until the meat is tender. Stir in the peanuts and chile and serve with rice.

spicy beef with potato

ingredients

SERVES 4

1 lb/400 g beef fillet
2 tbsp Thai soy sauce
2 tbsp fish sauce
2 tbsp vegetable or peanut oil
3–4 cilantro roots, chopped
1 tbsp crushed black
    peppercorns
2 garlic cloves, chopped
1 tbsp jaggery or soft light
    brown sugar
12 oz/350 g potatoes, diced
5 fl oz/150 ml/^{2}/$_3$ cup water
bunch of scallions, chopped
8 oz/225 g/5 cups baby
    spinach leaves
cooked rice or noodles, to serve

method

1 Cut the beef into thick slices and place in a shallow dish. Put the soy sauce, fish sauce, 1 tablespoon of the oil, the cilantro roots, peppercorns, garlic, and sugar in a food processor and process to a thick paste. Scrape the paste into the dish and toss the beef to coat. Cover with plastic wrap and set aside to marinate in the refrigerator for at least 3 hours, and preferably overnight.

2 Heat the remaining oil in a wok. Lift the beef out of the marinade, reserving the marinade, and cook for 3–4 minutes on each side, until browned. Add the reserved marinade and the potatoes with the measured water and gradually bring to a boil. Let simmer for 6–8 minutes, or until the potatoes are tender.

3 Add the scallions and spinach. Cook gently until the greens have wilted. Serve immediately with rice or noodles.

beef chop suey

ingredients

SERVES 4

1 lb/450 g ribeye or sirloin
  steak, finely sliced
1 head broccoli, cut into
  small florets
2 tbsp vegetable or peanut oil
1 onion, finely sliced
2 celery stalks, finely sliced
  diagonally
8 oz/225 g/2 cups snow peas,
  sliced in half lengthwise
2 oz/55 g/$^1/_2$ cup fresh or
  canned bamboo shoots,
  rinsed and julienned (if
  using fresh shoots, boil in
  water first for 30 minutes)
8 water chestnuts, finely sliced
8 oz/225 g/4 cups finely
  sliced mushrooms
1 tbsp oyster sauce
1 tsp salt
cooked rice, to serve

marinade

1 tbsp Shaoxing rice wine
pinch of white pepper
pinch of salt
1 tbsp light soy sauce
$^1/_2$ tsp sesame oil

method

1 Combine all the marinade ingredients
in a bowl and marinate the beef for at least
20 minutes. Blanch the broccoli in a large
pan of boiling water for 30 seconds. Drain
and set aside.

2 In a preheated wok, heat 1 tablespoon of
the oil and stir-fry the beef until the color has
changed. Remove and set aside.

3 In the clean wok, heat the remaining oil and
stir-fry the onion for 1 minute. Add the celery
and broccoli and cook for 2 minutes. Add the
snow peas, bamboo shoots, chestnuts, and
mushrooms and cook for 1 minute. Add the
beef, then season with the oyster sauce and
salt and serve.

beef with onions & broccoli

ingredients

SERVES 4

2 tbsp vegetable or peanut oil

2 tbsp Thai green curry paste

2 x 6-oz/175-g sirloin steaks,
    sliced thinly

2 onions, sliced

6 scallions, chopped

2 shallots, chopped finely

8 oz/225 g head broccoli,
    cut into florets

14 fl oz/400 ml/1¾ cups
    coconut milk

3 kaffir lime leaves, chopped
    coarsely

4 tbsp chopped fresh cilantro

few Thai basil leaves

method

1 Heat the oil in a wok and stir-fry the curry paste for 1–2 minutes. Add the meat, in batches if necessary, and stir-fry until starting to brown.

2 Add the onions, scallions, and shallots, and stir-fry for 2–3 minutes. Add the broccoli and stir-fry for 2–3 minutes.

3 Pour in the coconut milk, add the lime leaves, and bring to a boil. Let simmer gently for 8–10 minutes, until the meat is tender. Stir in the cilantro and basil and serve immediately.

stir-fried beef with broccoli & ginger

ingredients

SERVES 4–6

12 oz/350 g tenderloin steak,
    cut into thin strips
6 oz/175 g broccoli florets
2 tbsp vegetable or peanut oil
1 garlic clove, finely chopped
1 tsp finely chopped fresh
    gingerroot
1 small onion, finely sliced
1 tsp salt
1 tsp light soy sauce

marinade

1 tbsp light soy sauce
1 tsp sesame oil
1 tsp Shaoxing rice wine
1 tsp sugar
pinch of white pepper

method

1 Combine the marinade ingredients in a bowl, then mix in the beef. Cover and let stand for 1 hour, basting occasionally. Blanch the broccoli in a large pan of boiling water for 30 seconds. Drain and set aside.

2 In a preheated wok, heat 1 tablespoon of the oil and stir-fry the garlic, gingerroot, and onion for 1 minute. Add the broccoli and stir-fry for an additional minute. Remove from the wok and set aside.

3 In the clean preheated wok, heat the remaining oil and stir-fry the beef until the color has changed. Return the broccoli mixture to the wok with the salt and light soy sauce and stir until cooked through. Serve immediately.

hot sesame beef

ingredients

SERVES 4

1 lb 2 oz/500 g beef fillet,
    cut into thin strips

1$^{1}/_{2}$ tbsp sesame seeds

4 fl oz/125 ml/$^{1}/_{2}$ cup
    beef stock

2 tbsp soy sauce

2 tbsp grated fresh gingerroot

2 garlic cloves, chopped finely

1 tsp cornstarch

$^{1}/_{2}$ tsp chile flakes

3 tbsp sesame oil

1 large head of broccoli,
    cut into florets

1 orange bell pepper,
    sliced thinly

1 red chile, seeded and
    sliced finely

1 tbsp chili oil, to taste

cooked long-grain and wild
    rice, to serve

1 tbsp chopped fresh cilantro,
    to garnish

method

1 Mix the beef strips with 1 tablespoon of the sesame seeds in a small bowl. In a separate bowl, whisk together the beef stock, soy sauce, gingerroot, garlic, cornstarch, and chile flakes.

2 Heat 1 tablespoon of the sesame oil in a wok. Stir-fry the beef strips for 2–3 minutes. Remove and set aside.

3 Discard any oil remaining in the wok, then wipe with paper towels to remove any stray sesame seeds. Heat the remaining oil and add the broccoli, orange bell pepper, chile and chili oil (if desired), then stir-fry for 2–3 minutes. Stir in the beef bouillon mixture, then cover and simmer for 2 minutes.

4 Return the beef to the wok and simmer until the juices thicken, stirring occasionally. Cook for another 1–2 minutes.

5 Sprinkle with the remaining sesame seeds. Serve over cooked long-grain and wild rice and garnish with fresh cilantro.

ma po doufu

ingredients

SERVES 4

1 lb/450 g bean curd

2 tbsp vegetable or peanut oil

1 tsp Sichuan peppers

3 1/2 oz/100 g/scant 1 cup
  ground beef

2 tbsp chili bean sauce

1 tsp fermented black beans,
  rinsed and lightly mashed

3 1/2 fl oz/100 ml/1 1/4 cups
  hot chicken stock

pinch of sugar

1 tsp light soy sauce

pinch of salt

2 tbsp thinly sliced scallion,
  cut on the diagonal

method

1 Cut the bean curd into 3/4-inch/2-cm cubes and arrange in a large pan. Pour over enough boiling water to cover and let rest.

2 In a preheated wok, heat the oil until almost smoking. Throw in the Sichuan peppers and stir until fragrant. Add the beef and stir-fry until brown and crispy.

3 Lower the heat and add the chili bean sauce and black beans and stir for about 30 seconds, or until the oil is richly red.

4 Pour in the hot chicken stock and gently add the drained bean curd. Season with the sugar, light soy sauce, and salt. Simmer for about 5 minutes.

5 Finally, toss in the scallion. Transfer into 1 large or 4 individual bowls and serve.

katsudon

ingredients

SERVES 4

4 tbsp all-purpose flour

1 egg, lightly beaten

4 oz/115 g/generous $2^{1}/_{4}$
    cups Tonkatsu (panko)
    bread crumbs

4 pork chops, about $5^{1}/_{2}$ oz/
    150 g each, bones removed

oil, for pan-frying

1 pint/600 ml/scant $2^{1}/_{2}$ cups
    dashi stock

4 tbsp shoyu (Japanese
    soy sauce)

2 tbsp mirin

1 onion, sliced

4 eggs

1 lb 5 oz/600 g cooked
    Japanese short-grain rice

method

1 Put the flour, egg, and bread crumbs separately into 3 shallow bowls large enough to fit a pork chop. Roll a rolling pin over each chop to thin it a little.

2 Dip each chop first in the flour, then in the egg, and finally in the bread crumbs to coat. Cover with plastic wrap and let chill in the refrigerator for 10 minutes, then dip again in the egg and bread crumbs.

3 Preheat a wok over high heat. Add oil to a depth of about $^{3}/_{4}$ inch/2 cm and heat until very hot. Add the chops, one at a time, reduce the heat to medium, and cook for 4 minutes on each side, or until the pork is cooked through and the bread crumbs are golden. Remove and slice.

4 Meanwhile, put the stock, soy sauce, and mirin in a pan and bring to a simmer. Add the onion and let simmer for 5 minutes. Beat the eggs in a bowl, then pour over the onions in the stock. Cover and cook for 1 minute.

5 Divide the rice between 4 bowls. Lay the pork slices on top, then ladle some of the egg, onion, and stock over the pork and rice. Serve immediately.

spicy sichuan pork

ingredients

SERVES 4

10 oz/280 g pork belly, thinly
    sliced

1 tbsp vegetable or peanut oil

1 tbsp chili bean sauce

1 tbsp fermented black beans,
    rinsed and lightly mashed

1 tsp sweet red bean paste
    (optional)

1 green bell pepper, finely
    sliced

1 red bell pepper, finely sliced

1 tsp sugar

1 tsp dark soy sauce

pinch of white pepper

cooked rice, to serve

method

1 If cooking the pork especially for this dish,
bring a pan of water to a boil and place the
pork in the pan, then cover and simmer for
about 20 minutes, skimming occasionally. Let
the pork cool and rest before slicing thinly.

2 In a preheated wok, heat the oil and stir-fry
the pork slices until they begin to shrink. Stir
in the chili bean sauce, then add the black
beans and the red bean paste, if using.
Finally, toss in the bell peppers and the
remaining ingredients and stir-fry for a couple
of minutes.

hoisin pork with garlic noodles

ingredients

SERVES 4

9 oz/250 g dried thick Chinese
egg noodles, or Chinese
wholemeal egg noodles

1 lb/450 g pork fillet, thinly
sliced

1 tsp sugar

1 tbsp peanut or corn oil

4 tbsp rice vinegar

4 tbsp white wine vinegar

4 tbsp bottled hoisin sauce

2 scallions, sliced on the
diagonal

about 2 tbsp garlic-flavored
corn oil

2 large garlic cloves, thinly
sliced

chopped fresh cilantro,
to garnish

method

1 Start by boiling the noodles for 3 minutes, until soft. Alternatively, cook according to the package instructions. Drain well, rinse under cold water to stop the cooking, and drain again, then set aside.

2 Meanwhile, sprinkle the pork slices with the sugar and use your hands to toss together. Heat a wok over high heat. Add the oil and heat until it shimmers. Add the pork and stir-fry for about 3 minutes, until the pork is cooked through and is no longer pink. Use a slotted spoon to remove the pork from the wok and keep warm. Add both vinegars to the wok and boil until they are reduced to about 5 tablespoons. Pour in the hoisin sauce with the scallions and let bubble until reduced by half. Add to the pork and stir together.

3 Quickly wipe out the wok and reheat. Add the garlic-flavored oil and heat until it shimmers. Add the garlic slices and stir round for about 30 seconds, until they are golden and crisp, then use a slotted spoon to scoop them out of the wok and set aside.

4 Add the noodles to the wok and stir them round to warm them through. Divide the noodles between 4 plates, top with the pork and onion mixture, and sprinkle over the garlic slices and cilantro.

pork & crab meatballs

ingredients

SERVES 6

8 oz/225 g pork fillet,
    chopped finely

5³/₄ oz/170 g canned
    crabmeat, drained

3 scallions, chopped finely

1 garlic clove, chopped finely

1 tsp Thai red curry paste

1 tbsp cornstarch

1 egg white

vegetable or peanut oil,
    for deep-frying

boiled rice, to serve

sauce

1 tbsp vegetable or peanut oil

2 shallots, chopped

1 garlic clove, crushed

2 large fresh red chilies,
    seeded and chopped

4 scallions, chopped

3 tomatoes, chopped coarsely

method

1 Put the pork and crabmeat into a bowl and mix together. Add the scallions, garlic, curry paste, cornstarch, and egg white, and beat well to make a thick paste. With damp hands shape the mixture into walnut-size balls.

2 Heat the oil in a wok and deep-fry the balls, in batches, for 3–4 minutes, turning frequently, until golden brown and cooked. Drain on paper towels and keep warm.

3 To make the sauce, heat the oil in a wok and stir-fry the shallots and garlic for 1–2 minutes. Add the chilies and scallions and stir-fry for 1–2 minutes, then add the tomatoes. Stir together quickly, then spoon the sauce over the pork and crab balls. Serve immediately with rice.

pork with bell peppers

ingredients

SERVES 4

1 tbsp vegetable or peanut oil

1 tbsp chili oil

1 lb pork fillet, sliced thinly

2 tbsp green chili sauce

6 scallions, sliced

1-inch piece fresh gingerroot,
    sliced thinly

1 red bell pepper, seeded
    and sliced

1 yellow bell pepper, seeded
    and sliced

1 orange bell pepper, seeded
    and sliced

1 tbsp fish sauce

2 tbsp Thai soy sauce

juice of $1/2$ lime

4 tbsp chopped fresh parsley

cooked flat rice noodles,
    to serve

method

1 Heat both the oils in a wok. Add the pork, in batches, and stir-fry until browned all over. Remove with a slotted spoon and set aside.

2 Add the chili sauce, scallions, and gingerroot to the wok and stir-fry for 1–2 minutes. Add the bell peppers and stir–fry for 2–3 minutes.

3 Return the meat to the wok, stir well, and add the fish sauce, soy sauce, and lime juice. Cook for an additional 1–2 minutes, then stir in the parsley and serve with flat rice noodles.

spareribs in a sweet-&-sour sauce

ingredients

SERVES 4

1 lb/450 g spareribs, cut into
  bite-size pieces (you or
  your butcher can cut ribs
  into pieces with a cleaver)
vegetable or peanut oil,
  for deep-frying

marinade

2 tsp light soy sauce
$^1/_2$ tsp salt
pinch of white pepper

sauce

3 tbsp white rice vinegar
2 tbsp sugar
1 tbsp light soy sauce
1 tbsp tomato ketchup
$1^1/_2$ tbsp vegetable or peanut oil
1 green bell pepper, coarsely
  chopped
1 small onion, coarsely chopped
1 small carrot, finely sliced
$^1/_2$ tsp finely chopped garlic
$^1/_2$ tsp finely chopped
  gingerroot
$3^1/_2$ oz/100 g pineapple chunks

method

1 Combine the marinade ingredients in a bowl with the pork and let marinate for at least 20 minutes.

2 Heat enough oil for deep-frying in a wok or deep-fat fryer until it reaches 350–375°F/180–190°C, or until a cube of bread browns in 30 seconds. Deep-fry the spareribs for 8 minutes. Drain and set aside.

3 To prepare the sauce, first mix together the vinegar, sugar, light soy sauce, and ketchup. Set aside.

4 In a preheated wok, heat 1 tablespoon of the oil and stir-fry the bell pepper, onion, and carrot for 2 minutes. Remove and set aside.

5 In the clean preheated wok, heat the remaining oil and stir-fry the garlic and gingerroot until fragrant. Add the vinegar mixture. Bring back to a boil and add the pineapple chunks. Finally add the spareribs and the bell pepper, onion, and carrot. Stir until warmed through and serve immediately.

chicken with cashew nuts

ingredients

SERVES 4–6

1 lb/450 g boneless chicken
    meat, cut into bite-size
    pieces
3 tbsp light soy sauce
1 tsp Shaoxing rice wine
pinch of sugar
$1/2$ tsp salt
3 dried Chinese mushrooms,
    soaked in warm water for
    20 minutes
2 tbsp vegetable or peanut oil
4 slices of fresh gingerroot
1 tsp finely chopped garlic
1 red bell pepper, cut into
    1-inch/2.5-cm squares
3 oz/85 g/generous $1/2$ cup
    cashew nuts, roasted

method

1 Marinate the chicken in 2 tablespoons of the light soy sauce, Shaoxing, sugar, and salt for at least 20 minutes.

2 Squeeze any excess water from the mushrooms and finely slice, discarding any tough stems. Reserve the soaking water.

3 In a preheated wok, heat 1 tablespoon of the oil. Add the gingerroot and stir-fry until fragrant. Stir in the chicken and cook for 2 minutes, or until it begins to turn brown. Before the chicken is cooked through, remove and set aside.

4 In the clean wok, heat the remaining oil and stir-fry the garlic until fragrant. Add the mushrooms and red bell pepper and stir-fry for 1 minute. Add about 2 tablespoons of the mushroom soaking water and cook for about 2 minutes, or until the water has evaporated.

5 Return the chicken to the wok, then add the remaining light soy sauce and the cashew nuts and stir-fry for 2 minutes, or until the chicken is cooked through.

chicken with water chestnuts with plum sauce

ingredients

MAKES 6

1 tbsp vegetable or peanut oil

3^1/$_2$ oz/100 g chicken, finely chopped

1 oz/25 g water chestnuts, finely chopped

1 tsp finely chopped Chinese chives

1 oz/25 g pine nuts, lightly toasted

1 tsp salt

^{1}/$_2$ tsp white pepper

6 lettuce leaves, washed

3 tsp plum sauce, to serve

method

1 In a preheated wok, heat the oil and stir-fry the chicken for 1 minute. Add the water chestnuts and chives and cook for 2 minutes. Add the pine nuts and cook for 1 minute. Add the salt and pepper and stir.

2 To serve, place a spoonful in the center of each lettuce leaf, then top with the plum sauce and fold the lettuce leaf to make a small roll.

sweet-&-sour chicken

ingredients

SERVES 4–6

1 lb/450 g lean chicken meat, cubed

5 tbsp vegetable or peanut oil

$1/2$ tsp minced garlic

$1/2$ tsp finely chopped fresh gingerroot

1 green bell pepper, coarsely chopped

1 onion, coarsely chopped

1 carrot, finely sliced

1 tsp sesame oil

1 tbsp finely chopped scallion

marinade

2 tsp light soy sauce

1 tsp Shaoxing rice wine

pinch of white pepper

$1/2$ tsp salt

dash of sesame oil

sauce

8 tbsp rice vinegar

4 tbsp sugar

2 tsp light soy sauce

6 tbsp tomato ketchup

method

1 Place all the marinade ingredients in a bowl and marinate the chicken pieces for at least 20 minutes.

2 To prepare the sauce, heat the vinegar in a pan and add the sugar, light soy sauce, and tomato ketchup. Stir to dissolve the sugar, then set aside.

3 In a preheated wok, heat 3 tablespoons of the oil and stir-fry the chicken until it starts to turn golden brown. Remove and set aside.

4 In the clean wok, heat the remaining oil and cook the garlic and gingerroot until fragrant. Add the vegetables and cook for 2 minutes. Add the chicken and cook for 1 minute. Finally add the sauce and sesame oil, then stir in the scallion and serve.

gong bau chicken

ingredients

SERVES 4

2 boneless chicken breasts,
with or without skin, cut
into $1/2$-inch/1-cm cubes

1 tbsp vegetable or peanut oil

10 dried red chiles or more,
to taste, snipped into
2 or 3 pieces

1 tsp Sichuan peppers

3 garlic cloves, finely sliced

1-inch/2.5-cm piece of fresh
gingerroot, finely sliced

1 tbsp coarsely chopped
scallion, white part only

3 oz/85 g/generous $1/2$ cup
peanuts, roasted

marinade

2 tsp light soy sauce

1 tsp Shaoxing rice wine

$1/2$ tsp sugar

sauce

1 tsp light soy sauce

1 tsp dark soy sauce

1 tsp black Chinese rice vinegar

a few drops of sesame oil

2 tbsp chicken stock

1 tsp sugar

method

1 Combine all the ingredients for the marinade in a bowl and marinate the chicken, covered, for at least 20 minutes. Combine all the ingredients for the sauce and set aside.

2 In a preheated wok, heat the oil and stir-fry the chiles and peppers until crisp and fragrant. Toss in the chicken pieces. When they begin to turn white, add the garlic, gingerroot, and scallion. Stir-fry for about 5 minutes, or until the chicken is cooked.

3 Pour in the sauce, mix together thoroughly, then stir in the peanuts. Serve immediately.

green chicken curry

ingredients

SERVES 4

1 tbsp vegetable or peanut oil

1 onion, sliced

1 garlic clove, chopped finely

2–3 tbsp Thai green
curry paste

14 fl oz/400 ml/1³/₄ cups
coconut milk

5 fl oz/150 ml/²/₃ cup
chicken stock

4 kaffir lime leaves

4 skinless, boneless chicken
breasts, cut into cubes

1 tbsp fish sauce

2 tbsp Thai soy sauce

grated rind and juice of
¹/₂ lime

1 tsp jaggery or soft light
brown sugar

4 tbsp chopped fresh cilantro,
to garnish

method

1 Heat the oil in a wok and stir-fry the onion and garlic for 1–2 minutes, until starting to soften. Add the curry paste and stir-fry for 1–2 minutes.

2 Add the coconut milk, stock, and lime leaves, bring to a boil and add the chicken. Reduce the heat and let simmer gently for 15–20 minutes, until the chicken is tender.

3 Add the fish sauce, soy sauce, lime rind and juice, and sugar. Cook for 2–3 minutes, until the sugar has dissolved. Serve immediately, garnished with chopped cilantro.

chicken with yellow curry sauce

ingredients

SERVES 4

spice paste

6 tbsp Thai yellow
    curry paste
5 fl oz/150 ml/^{2}/$_3$ cup
    plain yogurt
14 fl oz/400 ml/1^3/$_4$ cups
    water
handful of fresh cilantro,
    chopped
handful of fresh Thai basil
    leaves, shredded

stir-fry

2 tbsp vegetable or peanut oil
2 onions, cut into thin wedges
2 garlic cloves, chopped finely
2 skinless, boneless chicken
    breasts, cut into strips
6 oz/175 g baby corn, halved
    lengthwise
chopped fresh cilantro
shredded fresh basil,
    to garnish

method

1 To make the spice paste, stir-fry the yellow curry paste in a wok for 2–3 minutes, then stir in the yogurt, water, and herbs. Bring to a boil, then let simmer for 2–3 minutes.

2 Meanwhile, heat the oil in a wok and stir-fry the onions and garlic for 2–3 minutes. Add the chicken and corn and stir-fry for 3–4 minutes, until the meat and corn are tender.

3 Stir in the spice paste and bring to a boil. Let simmer for 2–3 minutes, until heated through. Serve immediately, garnished with extra herbs if desired.

gingered chicken & vegetable salad

ingredients

SERVES 4

4 skinless, boneless chicken
  breasts
4 scallions, chopped
1-inch piece fresh gingerroot,
  chopped finely
2 garlic cloves, crushed
2 tbsp vegetable or peanut oil

salad

1 tbsp vegetable or peanut oil
1 onion, sliced
2 garlic cloves, chopped
4 oz/115 g baby corn, halved
4 oz/115 g snow peas, halved
  lengthwise
1 red bell pepper, seeded
  and sliced
3-inch piece cucumber,
  peeled, seeded, and sliced
4 tbsp Thai soy sauce
1 tbsp jaggery or soft light
  brown sugar
few Thai basil leaves
6 oz/175 g fine egg noodles

method

1 Cut the chicken into large cubes, each about 1 inch. Mix the scallions, gingerroot, garlic, and oil together in a shallow dish and add the chicken. Cover and let marinate for at least 3 hours. Lift the meat out of the marinade and set aside.

2 Heat the oil in a wok and cook the onion for 1–2 minutes before adding the rest of the vegetables except the cucumber. Cook for 2–3 minutes, until just tender. Add the cucumber, half the soy sauce, the sugar, and the basil, and mix gently.

3 Soak the noodles for 2–3 minutes (check the package instructions) or until tender, and drain well. Sprinkle the remaining soy sauce over them and arrange on plates. Top with the cooked vegetables.

4 Add a little more oil to the wok if necessary and cook the chicken over fairly high heat until browned on all sides. Arrange the chicken cubes on top of the salad and serve hot or warm.

red chicken salad

ingredients

SERVES 4

4 boneless chicken breasts

2 tbsp Thai red curry paste

2 tbsp vegetable or peanut oil

1 head Napa cabbage,
　shredded

6 oz/175 g bok choy, torn into
　large pieces

1/2 savoy cabbage, shredded

2 shallots, chopped finely

2 garlic cloves, crushed

1 tbsp rice wine vinegar

2 tbsp sweet chili sauce

2 tbsp Thai soy sauce

method

1 Slash the flesh of the chicken several times and rub the curry paste into each cut. Cover and let chill overnight.

2 Cook in a wok over medium heat for 5–6 minutes, turning once or twice, until cooked through. Keep warm.

3 Heat 1 tablespoon of the oil in a wok and stir-fry the cabbage and bok choy until just wilted. Add the remaining oil, shallots, and garlic, and stir-fry until just tender but not browned. Add the vinegar, chili sauce, and soy. Remove from the heat.

4 Arrange the leaves on 4 serving plates. Slice the chicken, arrange on the salad greens, and drizzle the hot dressing over. Serve immediately.

turkey with bamboo shoots & water chestnuts

ingredients

SERVES 4

marinade

4 tbsp sweet sherry

1 tbsp lemon juice

1 tbsp soy sauce

2 tsp grated fresh gingerroot

1 clove garlic, crushed

stir-fry

1 tbsp sesame oil

2 tbsp vegetable oil

1 lb/450 g turkey breast, cubed

125 g/4^{1}/$_{2}$ oz small mushrooms, cut into halves

1 green bell pepper, cut into strips

1 zucchini, sliced thinly

4 scallions, cut into fourths

4 oz/115 g canned bamboo shoots, drained

4 oz/115 g canned sliced water chestnuts, drained

cooked noodles or rice, to serve

method

1 Blend the sherry, lemon juice, soy sauce, gingerroot, and garlic in a bowl, then add the turkey and stir. Cover the dish with plastic wrap and refrigerate to marinate for 3–4 hours.

2 In a wok, add the sesame oil and vegetable oil and heat slowly. Remove the turkey from the marinade with a slotted spoon (reserving the marinade) and stir-fry a few pieces at a time until browned. Remove the turkey from the wok and set aside.

3 Add the mushrooms, green bell pepper, and zucchini to the wok and stir-fry for 3 minutes. Add the scallions and stir-fry for 1 minute more. Add the bamboo shoots and water chestnuts to the wok, then the turkey along with half of the reserved marinade. Stir over a medium–high heat for another 2–3 minutes, or until the ingredients are evenly coated and the marinade has reduced.

4 Serve immediately over noodles or rice.

duck with mixed bell peppers

ingredients

SERVES 4

1 tbsp vegetable or peanut oil

2 duck breasts, skin on

1 onion, sliced

2 garlic cloves, chopped

1 red bell pepper, seeded and
    chopped

1 green bell pepper, seeded
    and chopped

1 yellow bell pepper, seeded
    and chopped

4 tomatoes, peeled, seeded,
    and chopped

5 fl oz/150 ml/$^2/_3$ cup stock

3 tbsp Thai soy sauce

boiled noodles, garnished
    with chopped scallion,
    to serve

method

1 Heat the oil in a wok and cook the duck breasts over high heat until crisp and brown. Turn over and cook until cooked through. Lift out and keep warm.

2 Pour off any excess fat and stir-fry the onion and garlic for 2–3 minutes, until softened and lightly browned.

3 Add the bell peppers and stir-fry for 2–3 minutes, until tender. Add the tomatoes, stock, and soy sauce, and let simmer for 1–2 minutes. Transfer to a serving plate. Slice the duck thickly and arrange on top, spooning any sauce over it. Serve with noodles.

duck salad

ingredients

SERVES 4

4 boneless duck breasts,
  skin on
1 lemongrass stalk, broken
  into three and each cut in
  half lengthwise
3 tbsp vegetable or peanut oil
2 tbsp sesame oil
1 tsp fish sauce
1 fresh green chile, seeded
  and chopped
2 tbsp Thai red curry paste
$1/2$ fresh pineapple, peeled
  and sliced
3-inch piece cucumber,
  peeled, seeded, and sliced
3 tomatoes, cut into wedges
1 onion, sliced thinly

dressing

juice of 1 lemon
2 garlic cloves, crushed
1 tsp jaggery or soft light
  brown sugar
2 tbsp vegetable or peanut oil

method

1 Unwrap the duck and let the skin dry out overnight in the refrigerator.

2 The following day, slash the skin side 5 or 6 times. Mix the lemongrass, 2 tablespoons of the vegetable or peanut oil, all the sesame oil, fish sauce, chile, and curry paste together in a shallow dish and place the duck breasts in the mixture. Turn to coat and to rub the marinade into the meat. Let chill for 2–3 hours.

3 Heat the remaining oil in a wok and cook the duck, skin-side down, over medium heat for 3–4 minutes until the skin is browned and crisp and the meat cooked most of the way through. Turn the breasts over and cook until browned and the meat is cooked to your liking.

4 Meanwhile, arrange the pineapple, cucumber, tomatoes, and onions on a platter. Mix the dressing ingredients together and pour over the top.

5 Lift the duck out of the wok and slice thickly. Arrange the duck slices on top of the salad and serve while still hot.

fish & seafood

Fish and seafood are in plentiful supply in East Asia, so play an important role in the diet. They are given a similar treatment to meat and poultry, being cooked rapidly in a wok—steamed, deep-fried, or stir-fried—with plenty of flavorings or a sauce added.

If you think of fish as being sometimes rather bland, you will soon change your mind when you try the recipes in this section—it takes on a new excitement when cooked, for example, with a lime and chili sauce, or in a curry sauce. Or try Japanese-style fish cake, served with thick, round Udon noodles.

Choose fresh fish and cook it as soon as possible for the best flavor and quality. Recipes can be adapted to suit whatever fish is at its best, as long as it is from a similar "family" to the variety specified. Fish can be quite delicate, so treat it gently, especially when you are adding a sauce—the flesh should keep its shape and texture, and not disintegrate, so it is often cooked separately, removed from the wok, and added to the remaining ingredients just to be warmed through. Scallops and squid should always be cooked until just tender—overcooking will make them tough. And jumbo shrimp need to retain their firm texture—expensive and therefore treated with great respect in China, they are very special served in a spicy ginger sauce.

monkfish with lime & chile sauce

ingredients

SERVES 4

4 x 4-oz/115-g
   monkfish fillets

1 oz/25 g/¼ cup rice flour
   or cornstarch

6 tbsp vegetable or peanut oil

4 garlic cloves, crushed

2 large fresh red chiles,
   seeded and sliced

2 tsp jaggery or soft light
   brown sugar

juice of 2 limes

grated rind of 1 lime

boiled rice, to serve

method

1 Toss the fish in the flour, shaking off any excess. Heat the oil in a wok and cook the fish on all sides until browned and cooked through, taking care when turning not to break it up.

2 Lift the fish out of the wok and keep warm. Add the garlic and chiles and stir-fry for 1–2 minutes, until they have softened.

3 Add the sugar, the lime juice and rind, and 2–3 tablespoons of water and bring to a boil. Let simmer gently for 1–2 minutes, then spoon the mixture over the fish. Serve immediately with rice.

monkfish stir-fry

ingredients

SERVES 4

2 tsp sesame oil

1 lb/450 g monkfish steaks,
cut into 1 inch/
2.5 cm chunks

1 red onion, sliced thinly

3 cloves garlic, chopped
finely

1 tsp grated fresh gingerroot

8 oz/225 g fine tip asparagus

6 oz/185 g/3 cups
mushrooms, sliced thinly

2 tbsp soy sauce

1 tbsp lemon juice

lemon wedges, to garnish

cooked noodles, to serve

method

1 Heat the oil in a wok over a medium–high heat. Add the fish, onion, garlic, gingerroot, asparagus, and mushrooms. Stir-fry for 2–3 minutes.

2 Stir in the soy sauce and lemon juice and cook for another minute. Remove from the heat and transfer to warm serving dishes.

3 Garnish with lemon wedges and serve immediately on a bed of cooked noodles.

fried fish with pine nuts

ingredients

SERVES 4–6

$^1/_2$ tsp salt

1 lb/450 g thick white fish fillets,
   cut into 1-inch/2.5-cm
   cubes

2 dried Chinese mushrooms,
   soaked in warm water
   for 20 minutes

3 tbsp vegetable or peanut oil

1-inch/2.5-cm piece of fresh
   gingerroot, finely shredded

1 tbsp chopped scallion

1 red bell pepper, cut into
   1-inch/2.5-cm squares

1 green bell pepper, cut into
   1-inch/2.5-cm squares

25 g/1 oz fresh or canned
   bamboo shoots, rinsed
   and cut into small cubes
   (if using fresh shoots, boil
   in water first for 30 minutes)

2 tsp Shaoxing rice wine

2 tbsp pine nuts, toasted

cooked rice, to serve

method

1 Sprinkle the salt over the fish and set aside for 20 minutes. Squeeze out any excess water from the mushrooms and finely slice, discarding any tough stems.

2 In a preheated wok, heat 2 tablespoons of the oil and fry the fish for 3 minutes. Drain and set aside.

3 In the clean, preheated wok, heat the remaining oil and toss in the gingerroot. Stir until fragrant, then add the scallion, peppers, bamboo shoots, mushrooms, and Shaoxing and cook for 1–2 minutes.

4 Finally add the fish and stir to warm through. Sprinkle with pine nuts and serve.

fish in coconut

ingredients

SERVES 4

2 tbsp vegetable or peanut oil

6 scallions, chopped coarsely

1-inch/2.5-cm piece fresh
  gingerroot, grated

2–3 tbsp Thai red curry paste

14 fl oz/400 ml/1³/₄ cups
  coconut milk

5 fl oz/150 ml/²/₃ cup
  fish stock

4 kaffir lime leaves

1 lemongrass stalk, broken
  in half

12 oz/350 g white fish fillets,
  skinned and cut into
  chunks

8 oz/225 g squid rings and
  tentacles

8 oz/225 g large cooked
  shelled shrimp

1 tbsp fish sauce

2 tbsp Thai soy sauce

4 tbsp chopped fresh Chinese
  chives

boiled jasmine rice with
  chopped fresh cilantro,
  to serve

method

1 Heat the oil in a wok and stir-fry the scallions and gingerroot for 1–2 minutes. Add the curry paste and stir-fry for 1–2 minutes.

2 Add the coconut milk, fish stock, lime leaves, and lemongrass. Bring to a boil, then reduce the heat and let simmer for 1 minute.

3 Add the fish, squid, and shrimp, and let simmer for 2–3 minutes, until the fish is cooked. Add the fish and soy sauces and stir in the chives. Serve immediately with jasmine rice with fresh cilantro stirred through it.

chiles stuffed with fish paste

ingredients

SERVES 4–6

8 oz/225 g white fish, minced
2 tbsp lightly beaten egg
4–6 mild red and green chiles
vegetable or peanut oil, for
    shallow-frying
2 garlic cloves, finely chopped
$1/2$ tsp fermented black beans,
    rinsed and lightly mashed
1 tbsp light soy sauce
pinch of sugar
1 tbsp water

marinade

1 tsp finely chopped fresh
    gingerroot
pinch of salt
pinch of white pepper
$1/2$ tsp vegetable or peanut oil

method

1 Combine all the marinade ingredients in a bowl and marinate the fish for 20 minutes. Add the egg and mix by hand to create a smooth paste.

2 To prepare the chiles, cut in half lengthwise and scoop out the seeds and loose flesh. Cut into bite-size pieces. Spread each piece of chile with about $1/2$ teaspoon of the fish paste.

3 In a preheated wok, heat plenty of the oil and cook the chile pieces on both sides until beginning to turn golden brown. Drain and set aside.

4 Heat 1 tablespoon of the oil in the clean wok and stir-fry the garlic until aromatic. Stir in the black beans and mix well. Add the light soy sauce and sugar and stir, then add the chile pieces. Add the water, then cover and simmer over a low heat for 5 minutes. Serve immediately.

five-willow fish

ingredients

SERVES 4–6

1 whole sea bass or similar,
weighing 1–1$^{1}/_{2}$ lb/
450–675 g, gutted

2 tsp salt

6 tbsp vegetable or peanut oil

2 slices fresh gingerroot

2 garlic cloves, finely sliced

2 scallions, coarsely chopped

1 green bell pepper, thinly
sliced

1 red bell pepper, thinly
sliced

1 carrot, finely sliced

2 oz/55 g/$^{1}/_{2}$ cup fresh or
canned bamboo shoots,
rinsed and thinly sliced (if
using fresh shoots, boil in
water first for 30 minutes)

2 tomatoes, peeled, seeded,
and thinly sliced

1 tbsp Shaoxing rice wine

2 tbsp white rice vinegar

1 tbsp light soy sauce

1 tbsp sugar

method

1 Clean the fish and dry thoroughly. Score the fish on both sides with deep, diagonal cuts. Press $^{1}/_{2}$ teaspoon of the salt into the skin.

2 In a preheated wok, heat 4 tablespoons of the oil and cook the fish for about 4 minutes on each side, or until the flesh is soft. Drain, then set aside and keep warm.

3 In the clean preheated wok, heat the remaining oil and stir-fry the gingerroot, garlic, and scallions until fragrant. Toss in the vegetables with the remaining salt and stir rapidly for 2–3 minutes. Add the remaining ingredients and mix well for 2–3 minutes. Pour the sauce over the fish and serve at once.

fish curry

ingredients

SERVES 4

juice of 1 lime

4 tbsp fish sauce

2 tbsp Thai soy sauce

1 fresh red chile, seeded
   and chopped

12 oz/350 g monkfish fillet,
   cut into cubes

12 oz/350 g salmon fillets,
   skinned and cut into
   cubes

14 fl oz/400 ml/1^3/$_4$ cups
   coconut milk

3 kaffir lime leaves

1 tbsp Thai red curry paste

1 lemongrass stalk (white part
   only), chopped finely

2 cups jasmine rice, boiled

4 tbsp chopped fresh cilantro

method

1 Combine the lime juice, half the fish sauce, and the soy sauce in a shallow, nonmetallic dish. Add the chile and the fish, stir to coat, cover with plastic wrap, and chill for 1–2 hours, or overnight.

2 Bring the coconut milk to a boil in a wok and add the lime leaves, curry paste, the remaining fish sauce, and the lemongrass. Let simmer gently for 10–15 minutes.

3 Add the fish and the marinade and let simmer for 4–5 minutes, until the fish is cooked. Serve hot with boiled rice with chopped cilantro stirred through it.

mixed seafood curry

ingredients

SERVES 4

1 tbsp vegetable or peanut oil

3 shallots, chopped finely

1-inch piece fresh galangal,
  peeled and sliced thinly

2 garlic cloves, chopped finely

14 fl oz/400 ml/1¾ cups
  canned coconut milk

2 lemongrass stalks, snapped
  in half

4 tbsp fish sauce

2 tbsp chili sauce

8 oz/225 g uncooked jumbo
  shrimp, shelled

8 oz/225 g baby squid,
  cleaned and sliced thickly

8 oz/225 g salmon fillet,
  skinned and cut into
  chunks

6 oz/175 g tuna steak, cut
  into chunks

8 oz/225 g fresh mussels,
  scrubbed and debearded

fresh Chinese chives,
  to garnish

boiled rice, to serve

method

1 Heat the oil in a large wok and stir-fry the shallots, galangal, and garlic for 1–2 minutes, until they start to soften. Add the coconut milk, lemongrass, fish sauce, and chili sauce. Bring to a boil, reduce the heat, and let simmer for 1–2 minutes.

2 Add the prepared shrimp, squid, salmon, and tuna, and let simmer for 3–4 minutes, until the shrimp have turned pink and the fish is cooked.

3 Add the mussels to the wok and cover with a lid. Let simmer for 1–2 minutes, until they have opened. Discard any mussels that remain closed. Garnish with Chinese chives and serve immediately with rice.

spicy thai seafood stew

ingredients

SERVES 4

7 oz/200 g squid, cleaned
   and tentacles discarded

1 lb 2 oz/500 g firm white fish
   fillet, preferably monkfish
   or halibut

1 tbsp corn oil

4 shallots, finely chopped

2 garlic cloves, finely chopped

2 tbsp Thai green curry paste

2 small lemongrass stems,
   finely chopped

1 tsp shrimp paste

16 fl oz/500 ml/generous
   2 cups coconut milk

7 oz/200 g raw jumbo shrimp,
   shelled and deveined

12 live clams in shells, cleaned

8 fresh basil leaves, finely
   shredded

fresh basil leaves, to garnish

freshly cooked rice, to serve

method

1 Using a sharp knife, cut the squid body cavities into thick rings and the white fish into bite-size chunks.

2 Heat the oil in a large preheated wok. Add the shallots, garlic, and curry paste and stir-fry for 1–2 minutes. Add the lemongrass and shrimp paste, then stir in the coconut milk and bring to a boil.

3 Reduce the heat until the liquid is simmering gently, then add the white fish, squid, and shrimp to the wok and simmer for 2 minutes.

4 Add the clams and simmer for an additional 1 minute, or until the clams have opened. Discard any clams that remain closed.

5 Sprinkle the shredded basil leaves over the stew. Transfer to serving plates, then garnish with whole basil leaves and serve immediately with rice.

spicy scallops with lime & chile

ingredients

SERVES 4

16 large scallops, shelled
1 tbsp butter
1 tbsp vegetable oil
1 tsp crushed garlic
1 tsp grated fresh gingerroot
1 bunch of scallions,
    finely sliced
finely grated rind of 1 lime
1 small fresh red chile,
    seeded and very finely
    chopped
3 tbsp lime juice
lime wedges, to garnish
freshly cooked rice, to serve

method

1 Using a sharp knife, trim the scallops to remove any black intestine, then wash and pat dry with paper towels. Separate the corals from the white parts, then slice each white part in half horizontally, making 2 circles.

2 Heat the butter and oil in a preheated wok. Add the garlic and gingerroot and stir-fry for 1 minute without browning. Add the scallions and stir-fry for 1 minute.

3 Add the scallops and continue stir-frying over high heat for 4–5 minutes. Stir in the lime rind, chile, and lime juice and cook for an additional 1 minute.

4 Transfer the scallops to serving plates, then spoon over the cooking juices and garnish with lime wedges. Serve hot with freshly cooked rice.

stir-fried scallops with asparagus

ingredients

SERVES 4

8 oz/225 g scallops

2 tsp salt

8 oz/225 g asparagus

3 tbsp vegetable or peanut oil

2 oz/55 g/$^1/_2$ cup fresh or
   canned bamboo shoots,
   rinsed and thinly sliced (if
   using fresh shoots, boil in
   water first for 30 minutes)

1 small carrot, finely sliced

4 thin slices of fresh gingerroot

pinch of white pepper

2 tbsp Shaoxing rice wine

2 tbsp chicken stock

1 tsp sesame oil

method

1 Sprinkle the scallops with 1 teaspoon of the salt and let stand for 20 minutes.

2 Trim the asparagus, discarding the tough ends. Cut into 2-inch/5-cm pieces and blanch in a large pan of boiling water for 30 seconds. Drain and set aside.

3 In a preheated wok, heat 1 tablespoon of the oil and cook the scallops for 30 seconds. Drain and set aside.

4 In the clean wok, heat another tablespoon of the oil and stir-fry the asparagus, bamboo shoots, and carrot for 2 minutes. Season with the remaining salt. Drain and set aside.

5 In the clean wok, heat the remaining oil, then add the gingerroot and stir-fry until fragrant. Return the scallops and vegetables to the wok and sprinkle with the pepper, Shaoxing, and stock. Cover and continue cooking for 2 minutes, then toss through the sesame oil and serve.

scallops in black bean sauce

ingredients

SERVES 4

2 tbsp vegetable or peanut oil

1 tsp finely chopped garlic

1 tsp finely chopped fresh
gingerroot

1 tbsp fermented black beans,
rinsed and lightly mashed

14 oz/400 g scallops

$1/2$ tsp light soy sauce

1 tsp Shaoxing rice wine

1 tsp sugar

3–4 red Thai chiles, finely
chopped

1–2 tsp chicken stock

1 tbsp finely chopped scallion

method

1 In a preheated wok, heat the oil. Add the garlic and stir, then add the gingerroot and stir-fry together for about 1 minute, or until fragrant. Mix in the black beans, then toss in the scallops and stir-fry for 1 minute. Add the light soy sauce, Shaoxing, sugar, and chiles.

2 Lower the heat and simmer for 2 minutes, adding the stock if necessary. Finally add the scallion, then stir and serve.

squid & red bell peppers

ingredients

SERVES 4

spice paste

2 tbsp vegetable or peanut oil

1 tbsp chili oil with shrimp

2 shallots, chopped

2–3 large fresh red chilies,
seeded and chopped
coarsely

2 tbsp ground coriander

2 tbsp ground cumin

1-inch piece fresh gingerroot,
chopped

1 tbsp finely chopped
lemongrass

3–4 cilantro roots, chopped

1 tsp salt

1 tsp jaggery or soft light
brown sugar

stir-fry

2 red bell peppers, seeded
and diced

5 fl oz/150 ml/²/₃ cup
plain yogurt

1 lb 10 oz/750 g squid,
cleaned and sliced

juice of 1 lime

4 oz/115 g block creamed
coconut, chopped

5 fl oz/150 ml/²/₃ cup
hot water

cooked rice, to serve

method

1 Put all the ingredients for the spice paste into a food processor and process until chopped finely.

2 Scrape the spice paste into a wok and stir-fry gently for 3–4 minutes. Add the red bell peppers and stir-fry for 1–2 minutes.

3 Add the yogurt and bring to a boil. Add the squid and let simmer for 2–3 minutes, then stir in the lime juice, coconut, and water. Let simmer for an additional 1–2 minutes, until the coconut dissolves. Serve immediately.

stir-fried squid with hot black bean sauce

ingredients

SERVES 4

1 lb 10 oz/750 g squid,
    cleaned and tentacles
    discarded
1 large red bell pepper, seeded
4 oz/115 g/scant 1 cup
    snow peas
1 head bok choy
3 tbsp black bean sauce
1 tbsp Thai fish sauce
1 tbsp rice wine or dry sherry
1 tbsp dark soy sauce
1 tsp brown sugar
1 tsp cornstarch
1 tbsp water
1 tbsp corn oil
1 tsp sesame oil
1 small fresh red Thai chile,
    chopped
1 garlic clove, finely chopped
1 tsp grated fresh gingerroot
2 scallions, chopped

method

1 Cut the squid body cavities into fourths lengthwise. Use the tip of a small, sharp knife to score a diamond pattern into the flesh, without cutting all the way through. Pat dry with paper towels.

2 Cut the bell pepper into long, thin slices. Cut the snow peas in half diagonally. Coarsely shred the bok choy.

3 Mix the black bean sauce, fish sauce, rice wine, soy sauce, and sugar together in a bowl. Blend the cornstarch with the water and stir into the other sauce ingredients. Reserve the mixture until required.

4 Heat the oils in a preheated wok. Add the chile, garlic, gingerroot, and scallions and stir-fry for 1 minute. Add the bell pepper slices and stir-fry for 2 minutes.

5 Add the squid and stir-fry over high heat for an additional 1 minute. Stir in the snow peas and bok choy and stir for an additional 1 minute, or until wilted.

6 Stir in the sauce ingredients and cook, stirring constantly, for 2 minutes, or until the sauce thickens and clears. Serve immediately.

shrimp with scallions & straw mushrooms

ingredients

SERVES 4

2 tbsp vegetable or peanut oil

bunch of scallions, chopped

2 garlic cloves, chopped finely

6 oz/175 g block creamed
    coconut, chopped
    coarsely

2 tbsp Thai red curry paste

15 fl oz/450 ml/scant 2 cups
    fish stock

2 tbsp fish sauce

2 tbsp Thai soy sauce

6 sprigs fresh Thai basil

14 oz/400 g canned straw
    mushrooms, drained

12 oz/350 g large cooked
    shelled shrimp

boiled jasmine rice, to serve

method

1 Heat the oil in a wok and stir-fry the scallions and garlic for 2–3 minutes. Add the creamed coconut, red curry paste, and stock, and heat gently until the coconut has dissolved.

2 Stir in the fish sauce and soy sauce, then add the basil, mushrooms, and shrimp. Gradually bring to a boil and serve at once with jasmine rice.

shrimp fu yung

ingredients

SERVES 4–6

1 tbsp vegetable or peanut oil

4 oz/115 g raw shrimp,
    peeled and deveined

4 eggs, lightly beaten

1 tsp salt

pinch of white pepper

2 tbsp finely chopped
    Chinese chives

method

1 In a preheated wok, heat the oil and stir-fry the shrimp until they begin to turn pink.

2 Season the beaten eggs with the salt and pepper and pour over the shrimp. Stir-fry for 1 minute, then add the chives.

3 Cook for an additional 4 minutes, stirring all the time, until the eggs are cooked through but still soft in texture, and serve immediately.

wok-fried jumbo shrimp in spicy sauce

ingredients

SERVES 4

3 tbsp vegetable or peanut oil

1 lb/450 g raw jumbo shrimp, deveined but unpeeled

2 tsp finely chopped fresh gingerroot

1 tsp finely chopped garlic

1 tbsp chopped scallion

2 tbsp chili bean sauce

1 tsp Shaoxing rice wine

1 tsp sugar

$1/2$ tsp light soy sauce

1–2 tbsp chicken stock

method

1 In a preheated wok, heat the oil, then toss in the shrimp and stir-fry over high heat for about 4 minutes. Arrange the shrimp on the sides of the wok out of the oil, then throw in the gingerroot and garlic and stir until fragrant. Add the scallion and chili bean sauce. Stir the shrimp into this mixture.

2 Lower the heat slightly and add the Shaoxing, sugar, light soy sauce, and a little chicken stock. Cover and cook for an additional minute. Serve immediately.

somen noodles with shrimp

ingredients

SERVES 2

16 raw shrimp, shelled
   and deveined
3 shiitake mushrooms,
   finely sliced
1/4 white or green cabbage,
   shredded
1 carrot, shredded
2 bundles of somen noodles
6 shiso leaves, shredded

dressing

4 tbsp oil
1 tbsp sesame seeds, toasted
4 fl oz/125 ml/1/2 cup
   Japanese rice vinegar
1 tbsp sugar
1 tbsp usukuchi shoyu
   (Japanese light soy sauce)
salt

method

1 To make the dressing, mix 3 tablespoons of the oil and all the remaining dressing ingredients together, with salt to taste, in a nonmetallic bowl.

2 Preheat a wok over high heat. Add the remaining oil and heat until very hot. Add the shrimp and cook, tossing occasionally, until they have turned pink.

3 Add the mushrooms to the wok and stir-fry for 1 minute, then add the cabbage and carrot and toss together. Remove from the heat and let cool.

4 Cook the noodles according to the package instructions, then drain. Put in a large bowl with the shrimp mixture. Add the dressing and toss well. Sprinkle with the shiso leaves and serve.

stir-fried fresh crab with ginger

ingredients

SERVES 4

3 tbsp vegetable or peanut oil

2 large fresh crabs, cleaned, broken into pieces and legs cracked with a cleaver

2 oz/55 g fresh gingerroot, julienned

3$^{1}/_{2}$ oz/100 g scallions, chopped into 2-inch/5-cm lengths

2 tbsp light soy sauce

1 tsp sugar

pinch of white pepper

method

1 In a preheated wok, heat 2 tablespoons of the oil and cook the crab over high heat for 3–4 minutes. Remove and set aside.

2 In the clean wok, heat the remaining oil, then toss in the gingerroot and stir until fragrant. Add the scallions, then stir in the crab pieces. Add the light soy sauce, sugar, and pepper. Cover and simmer for 1 minute and serve immediately.

clams in black bean sauce

ingredients

SERVES 4

2 lb/900 g small clams

1 tbsp vegetable or peanut oil

1 tsp finely chopped fresh
  gingerroot

1 tsp finely chopped garlic

1 tbsp fermented black beans,
  rinsed and coarsely
  chopped

2 tsp Shaoxing rice wine

1 tbsp finely chopped scallion

1 tsp salt (optional)

method

1 Start by washing the clams thoroughly. Then let the clams soak in clean water until it is time to drain them and toss them in the wok.

2 In a preheated wok, heat the oil and stir-fry the gingerroot and garlic until fragrant. Add the black beans and cook for 1 minute.

3 Over high heat, add the clams and Shaoxing and stir-fry for 2 minutes to mix everything together. Cover and cook for about 3 minutes. Add the scallion and salt, if necessary, and serve immediately.

udon noodle stir-fry with fish cake and ginger

ingredients

SERVES 2

2 x 5¹/₂-oz/150-g packs
  ready-to-wok udon
  noodles

1 leek, shredded

6 oz/175 g/1¹/₃ cups
  bean sprouts

8 shiitake mushrooms,
  finely sliced

2 pieces Japanese fish
  cake, sliced

12 raw shrimp, shelled
  and deveined

2 eggs, beaten

oil, for stir-frying

2 tbsp shoyu (Japanese
  soy sauce)

3 tbsp mirin

2 tbsp chopped fresh
  cilantro leaves

chili oil

sesame oil

2 scallions, finely sliced

2 tbsp shredded beni-shoga
  (red ginger), to serve

method

1 Rinse the noodles under cold running water to remove any oil and tip into a bowl.

2 Add the leek, bean sprouts, mushrooms, fish cake, shrimp, and eggs to the noodles and mix well to combine.

3 Preheat a wok over high heat. Add a little oil and heat until very hot. Add the noodle mixture and stir-fry until golden, and the shrimp have turned pink and are cooked through.

4 Add the soy sauce, mirin, and cilantro and toss together. Divide the noodles between 2 bowls, drizzle with the chili and sesame oils, and sprinkle over the scallions and beni-shoga. Serve immediately.

rice & noodles

Rice and noodles are the two staples of East Asian cuisine and form an excellent base for stir-fried dishes. Rice is grown in this region, and Thai people in particular consume huge quantities— it is estimated that, on average, each of them eats about 1 lb 2 oz/ 500 g every day.

Noodles are eaten by the Thais, Chinese, and Japanese alike and there is a remarkable range available. Some are made, like Italian pasta, from wheat, but they are also made from rice flour, buckwheat (which, unlike wheat, is not a grain but a nut), or ground mung beans. Each variety takes on a different appearance once cooked— "cellophane" or bean thread noodles, for example, made from mung beans, become glossy, while rice noodles, translucent when raw, turn a mat white.

Rice and noodles are naturally low in fat, so these recipes are perfect for those who are keeping an eye on their health. And if you have children who are fussy eaters, the solution must surely be to serve them a simple but hearty Chinese family dish with the most appealing name—"ants climbing a tree." It is said to have been so called because the pieces of ground meat cling to the noodles, resembling an army of ants on the march!

egg fu yung

ingredients

SERVES 4–6

2 eggs

$1/2$ tsp salt

pinch of white pepper

1 tsp melted butter

2 tbsp vegetable or peanut oil

1 tsp finely chopped garlic

1 small onion, finely sliced

1 green bell pepper, finely
    sliced

1 lb/450 g cooked rice, chilled

1 tbsp light soy sauce

1 tbsp finely chopped scallion

5 oz/140 g/1 cup bean
    sprouts, trimmed

2 drops of sesame oil

method

1 Beat the eggs with the salt and pepper. Heat the butter in a pan and pour in the eggs. Cook as an omelet, until set, then remove from the pan and cut into slivers.

2 In a preheated wok, heat the oil and stir-fry the garlic until fragrant. Add the onion and stir-fry for 1 minute, then add the green bell pepper and stir for 1 more minute. Stir in the rice and when the grains are separated, stir in the light soy sauce and cook for 1 minute.

3 Add the scallion and egg strips and stir well, then finally add the bean sprouts and sesame oil. Stir-fry for 1 minute and serve.

egg-fried rice

ingredients

SERVES 4

2 tbsp vegetable or peanut oil

12 oz/350 g cooked rice, chilled

1 egg, well beaten

method

1 Heat the oil in a preheated wok and stir-fry the rice for 1 minute, breaking it down as much as possible into individual grains.

2 Quickly add the egg, stirring, so as to coat each piece of rice. Stir until the egg is cooked and the rice, as far as possible, is in single grains. Serve immediately.

egg-fried rice with chicken

ingredients

SERVES 4

8 oz/225 g/generous 1 cup
  jasmine rice

3 skinless, boneless chicken
  breasts, cut into cubes

14 fl oz/400 ml/1³/₄ cups
  canned coconut milk

1³/₄ oz/50 g block creamed
  coconut, chopped

2–3 cilantro roots, chopped

thinly pared rind of 1 lemon

1 fresh green chile, seeded
  and chopped

3 fresh Thai basil leaves

1 tbsp fish sauce

1 tbsp oil

3 eggs, beaten

fresh chives

sprigs fresh cilantro,
  for the garnish

method

1 Cook the rice in boiling water for 12–15 minutes, drain well, then let cool and chill in the refrigerator overnight.

2 Put the chicken into a pan and cover with the coconut milk. Add the creamed coconut, cilantro roots, lemon rind, and chile, and bring to a boil. Let simmer for 8–10 minutes, until the chicken is tender. Remove from the heat. Stir in the basil and fish sauce.

3 Meanwhile, heat the oil in a wok and stir-fry the rice for 2–3 minutes. Pour in the eggs and stir until they have cooked and mixed with the rice. Line 4 small ovenproof bowls or ramekins with plastic wrap and pack with the rice. Turn out carefully onto serving plates and remove the plastic wrap. Garnish with long chives and sprigs of cilantro. Serve with the chicken.

egg-fried rice with vegetables & crispy onions

ingredients

SERVES 4

4 tbsp vegetable or peanut oil

2 garlic cloves, chopped finely

2 fresh red chilies, seeded
and chopped

4 oz/115 g mushrooms,
sliced

2 oz/50 g snow peas, halved

2 oz/50 g baby corn, halved

3 tbsp Thai soy sauce

1 tbsp jaggery or soft light
brown sugar

few Thai basil leaves

12 oz/350 g/3 cups rice,
cooked and cooled

2 eggs, beaten

2 onions, sliced

method

1 Heat half the oil in a wok and sauté the garlic and chilies for 2–3 minutes.

2 Add the mushrooms, snow peas, and corn, and stir-fry for 2–3 minutes before adding the soy sauce, sugar, and basil. Stir in the rice.

3 Push the mixture to one side of the wok and add the eggs to the bottom. Stir until lightly set before combining into the rice mixture.

4 Heat the remaining oil in another wok and sauté the onions until crispy and brown. Serve the rice topped with the onions.

dan dan mian

ingredients

SERVES 4

1 tbsp vegetable or peanut oil

1 large dried chile, seeded
and snipped into 3 pieces

$1/2$ tsp Sichuan peppers

$3^1/2$ oz/100 g/scant 1 cup
ground beef

2 tsp light soy sauce

$10^1/2$ oz/300 g fine white
noodles

1 tbsp roasted peanuts,
chopped

sauce

1 tbsp preserved vegetables

$1/2$ tsp Sichuan peppers,
lightly roasted and crushed

$3^1/2$ fl oz/100 ml/$1^1/4$ cups
chicken stock

1 tsp black Chinese vinegar

1 tsp chili oil

1 tsp dark soy sauce

1 tbsp light soy sauce

1 tbsp sesame paste

few drops of sesame oil

2 scallions, finely chopped

method

1 Heat the oil in a preheated wok and toss in the chile and peppers, then add the meat and stir rapidly. When the meat has changed color, add the light soy sauce and continue to cook until the meat is well browned. Carefully mix the sauce ingredients together and pour into 4 noodle bowls.

2 Cook the noodles according to the directions on the package. When cooked, drain and divide among the bowls.

3 Top with the meat mixture, then sprinkle with the roasted peanuts and serve at once. Mix well before eating.

beef chow mein

ingredients

SERVES 4

10 oz/280 g tenderloin steak,
    cut into slivers

8 oz/225 g dried egg noodles

2 tbsp vegetable or peanut oil

1 onion, finely sliced

1 green bell pepper,
    finely sliced

5 oz/140 g/1 cup bean
    sprouts, trimmed

1 tsp salt

pinch of sugar

2 tsp Shaoxing rice wine

2 tbsp light soy sauce

1 tbsp dark soy sauce

1 tbsp finely shredded scallion

marinade

1 tsp light soy sauce

dash of sesame oil

$1/2$ tsp Shaoxing rice wine

pinch of white pepper

method

1 Combine all the marinade ingredients in a bowl and marinate the beef for at least 20 minutes.

2 Cook the noodles according to the directions on the package. When cooked, rinse under cold water and set aside.

3 In a preheated wok, heat the oil and stir-fry the beef for about 1 minute, or until the meat has changed color, then add the onion and cook for 1 minute, followed by the bell pepper and bean sprouts. Evaporate off any water from the vegetables. Add the salt, sugar, Shaoxing, and soy sauces. Stir in the noodles and toss for 1 minute. Finally, stir in the scallion and serve.

fried rice with pork & shrimp

ingredients

SERVES 4

3 tsp vegetable or peanut oil

1 egg, lightly beaten

3^1/$_2$ oz/100 g raw shrimp,
    peeled, deveined and
    cut into 2 pieces

3^1/$_2$ oz/100 g cha siu, finely
    chopped

2 tbsp finely chopped scallion

7 oz/200 g cooked rice, chilled

1 tsp salt

method

1 In a preheated wok, heat 1 teaspoon of the oil and pour in the egg. Cook until scrambled. Remove and set aside.

2 Add the remaining oil and stir-fry the shrimp, cha siu, and scallion for about 2 minutes. Add the rice and salt, breaking up the rice into grains, and cook for an additional 2 minutes. Finally, stir in the cooked egg. Serve at once.

pork lo mein

ingredients

SERVES 4–6

6 oz/175 g boneless lean pork, shredded

8 oz/225 g egg noodles

1¹/₂ tbsp vegetable or peanut oil

2 tsp finely chopped garlic

1 tsp finely chopped fresh gingerroot

1 carrot, julienned

8 oz/225 g/4 cups finely sliced mushrooms

1 green bell pepper, thinly sliced

1 tsp salt

4 fl oz/175 ml/¹/₂ cup hot chicken stock

7 oz/200 g/1¹/₃ cups bean sprouts, trimmed

2 tbsp finely chopped scallion

marinade

1 tsp light soy sauce

dash of sesame oil

pinch of white pepper

method

1 Combine all the marinade ingredients in a bowl and marinate the pork for at least 20 minutes.

2 Cook the noodles according to the directions on the package. When cooked, drain and then set aside.

3 In a preheated wok, heat 1 teaspoon of the oil and stir-fry the pork until the color has changed. Remove and set aside.

4 In the clean wok, heat the remaining oil and stir-fry the garlic and gingerroot until fragrant. Add the carrot and cook for 1 minute, then add the mushrooms and cook for 1 minute. Toss in the pepper and cook for 1 minute. Add the pork, salt, and stock and heat through. Finally, toss in the noodles, followed by the bean sprouts, and stir well. Sprinkle with the scallion and serve.

shrimp with coconut rice

ingredients

SERVES 4

4 oz/115 g/1 cup dried
 Chinese mushrooms

2 tbsp vegetable or peanut oil

6 scallions, chopped

2 oz/55 g/scant $1/2$ cup dry
 unsweetened coconut

1 fresh green chile, seeded
 and chopped

8 oz/225 g/generous 1 cup
 jasmine rice

5 fl oz/150 ml/$2/3$ cup
 fish stock

14 fl oz/400 ml/1 $3/4$ cups
 coconut milk

12 oz/350 g cooked
 shelled shrimp

6 sprigs fresh Thai basil

method

1 Place the mushrooms in a small bowl, cover with hot water, and set aside to soak for 30 minutes. Drain, then cut off and discard the stalks and slice the caps.

2 Heat 1 tablespoon of the oil in a wok and stir-fry the scallions, coconut, and chile for 2–3 minutes, until lightly browned. Add the mushrooms and stir-fry for 3–4 minutes.

3 Add the rice and stir-fry for 2–3 minutes, then add the stock and bring to a boil. Reduce the heat and add the coconut milk. Let simmer for 10–15 minutes, until the rice is tender. Stir in the shrimp and basil, heat through, and serve.

rice with seafood & squid

ingredients

SERVES 4

2 tbsp vegetable or peanut oil

3 shallots, chopped finely

2 garlic cloves, chopped
finely

8 oz/225 g/generous 1 cup
jasmine rice

10 fl oz/300 ml/1^1/4 cups
fish stock

4 scallions, chopped

2 tbsp Thai red curry paste

8 oz/225 g baby squid,
cleaned and sliced thickly

8 oz/225 g white fish fillets,
skinned and cut into
cubes

8 oz/225 g salmon fillets,
skinned and cut into
cubes

4 tbsp chopped fresh cilantro

method

1 Heat 1 tablespoon of the oil in a wok and
stir-fry the shallots and garlic for 2–3 minutes,
until softened. Add the rice and stir-fry for
2–3 minutes.

2 Add a ladleful of the stock and let simmer,
adding more stock as needed, for 12–15
minutes, until tender. Transfer to a dish, let
cool, and chill overnight.

3 Heat the remaining oil in a wok and stir-fry
the scallions and curry paste for 2–3 minutes.
Add the squid and fish and stir-fry gently to
avoid breaking up the fish. Stir in the rice and
cilantro, heat through gently, and serve.

beef with fresh noodles

ingredients

SERVES 4

6 dried black cloud Chinese
    mushrooms
2 tbsp vegetable or peanut oil
2 x 8-oz/225-g sirloin steaks,
    sliced thickly
1 onion, cut into thin wedges
2 garlic cloves, chopped
1 green bell pepper, seeded
    and chopped
3 celery stalks, sliced
2 tbsp Thai green curry paste
10 fl oz/300 ml/1 $1/4$ cups
    beef stock
4 tbsp black bean sauce
8 oz/225 g fresh egg noodles
4 tbsp chopped fresh parsley

method

1 Put the dried mushrooms in a bowl, cover with boiling water, and let soak for 30 minutes. Drain, then break up any larger pieces.

2 Heat the oil in a wok and stir-fry the steak over high heat until browned. Add the mushrooms, onion, garlic, bell pepper, and celery, and stir-fry for 3–4 minutes. Add the curry paste, beef stock, and black bean sauce, and stir-fry for 2–3 minutes.

3 Meanwhile, cook the noodles in boiling water for 3–4 minutes, drain well, and stir into the wok. Sprinkle the parsley over and stir. Serve immediately.

rice noodles with beef in black bean sauce

ingredients

SERVES 4–6

8 oz/225 g rump steak, finely sliced

8 oz/225 g rice sticks

2–3 tbsp vegetable or peanut oil

1 small onion, finely sliced

1 green bell pepper, finely sliced

1 red bell pepper, finely sliced

2 tbsp black bean sauce

2–3 tbsp light soy sauce

marinade

1 tbsp dark soy sauce

1 tsp Shaoxing rice wine

$1/2$ tsp sugar

$1/2$ tsp white pepper

method

1 Combine all the marinade ingredients in a bowl and marinate the beef for at least 20 minutes.

2 Cook the rice sticks according to the directions on the package. When cooked, drain and set aside.

3 In a preheated wok, heat the oil and stir-fry the beef for 1 minute, or until the meat has changed color. Drain the meat and set aside.

4 Pour off any excess oil from the wok and stir-fry the onion and bell peppers for 1 minute. Add the black bean sauce and stir well, then pour in the light soy sauce. Toss the rice sticks in the vegetables and when fully incorporated, add the beef and stir until warmed through. Serve immediately.

ants climbing a tree

ingredients

SERVES 4–6

2 oz/55 g/^{1}/$_2$ cup ground beef

2 oz/55 g/^{1}/$_2$ cup ground pork

1 tbsp light soy sauce

pinch of salt

1 tbsp vegetable or peanut oil

1 tbsp chili bean paste

1 tsp dark soy sauce

6 fl oz/175 ml/^{3}/$_4$ cup hot
    chicken stock

5 oz/140 g beanthread noodles,
    soaked in warm water for
    20 minutes and drained

2 scallions, finely chopped

method

1 Combine the ground meats with 1 teaspoon of the light soy sauce and the salt.

2 In a preheated wok, heat the oil and cook the ground meats until beginning to brown. Add the chili paste and stir rapidly. Stir in the dark soy sauce.

3 Pour in the stock, noodles, and remaining light soy sauce. Cover the wok and simmer for about 8–10 minutes, or until the wok is quite dry. Shake the wok but do not stir. Toss in the scallions and serve.

sour & spicy pork

ingredients

SERVES 4

2 oz/55 g dried Chinese cloud
ear mushrooms

3¹/₂ oz/100 g baby corn,
halved lengthwise

2 tbsp honey

1 tbsp tamarind paste

4 tbsp boiling water

2 tbsp dark soy sauce

1 tbsp rice vinegar

2 tbsp peanut or corn oil

1 large garlic clove, very finely
chopped

¹/₂-inch/1-cm piece fresh
gingerroot, peeled and
very finely chopped

¹/₂ tsp dried red pepper
flakes, or to taste

12 oz/350 g pork fillet,
thinly sliced

4 scallions, thickly sliced on
the diagonal

1 green bell pepper, cored,
seeded, and sliced

9 oz/250 g fresh Hokkien
noodles

chopped fresh cilantro,
to garnish

method

1 Soak the mushrooms in enough boiling water to cover for 20 minutes, or until they are tender. Drain them well, then cut off and discard any thick stems, and slice the cups if they are large. Meanwhile, bring a large pan of lightly salted water to a boil, add the baby corn, and blanch for 3 minutes. Drain the corn and run it under cold running water to stop the cooking, then set aside. Put the honey and tamarind paste in a small bowl and stir in the water, stirring until the paste dissolves. Then stir in the soy sauce and rice vinegar and set aside.

2 Heat a wok over high heat. Add 1 tablespoon of the oil and heat until it shimmers. Add the garlic, gingerroot, and red pepper flakes and stir-fry for about 30 seconds. Add the pork and continue stir-frying for 2 minutes.

3 Add the remaining oil to the wok and heat. Add the scallions, bell pepper, mushrooms, and baby corn, along with the tamarind mixture, and stir-fry for an additional 2–3 minutes, until the pork is cooked through and the vegetables are tender, but still firm to the bite. Add the noodles and use 2 forks to mix all the ingredients together. When the noodles and sauce are hot, sprinkle with cilantro.

pad thai

ingredients

SERVES 4

8 oz/225 g thick rice-stick
    noodles
2 tbsp vegetable or peanut oil
2 garlic cloves, chopped
2 fresh red chilies, seeded
    and chopped
6 oz/175 g pork fillet,
    sliced thinly
4 oz/115 g uncooked shrimp,
    shelled and chopped
8 fresh Chinese chives,
    chopped
2 tbsp fish sauce
juice of 1 lime
2 tsp jaggery or soft light
    brown sugar
2 eggs, beaten
4 oz/115 g/¾ cup
    bean sprouts
4 tbsp chopped fresh cilantro
4 oz/115 g/¾ cup unsalted
    peanuts, chopped, plus
    extra to serve
crispy fried onions, to serve

method

1 Soak the noodles in warm water for 10 minutes, drain well, and set aside.

2 Heat the oil in a wok and stir-fry the garlic, chilies, and pork for 2–3 minutes. Add the shrimp to the wok and stir-fry for an additional 2–3 minutes.

3 Add the chives and noodles, then cover and cook for 1–2 minutes. Add the fish sauce, lime juice, sugar, and eggs. Cook, stirring and tossing constantly to mix in the eggs.

4 Stir in the bean sprouts, cilantro, and peanuts, and serve with small dishes of crispy fried onions and extra chopped peanuts.

noodle baskets with chicken lime salad

ingredients

SERVES 4

peanut or corn oil, for
    deep-frying
9 oz/250 g fresh thin or
    medium Chinese egg
    noodles

chicken-lime salad

6 tbsp sour cream
6 tbsp mayonnaise
1-inch/2.5-cm piece fresh
    gingerroot, peeled and
    grated
grated rind and juice of 1 lime
4 skinless, boneless chicken
    thighs, poached and cooled,
    then cut into thin strips
1 carrot, peeled and grated
1 cucumber, cut in half
    lengthwise, seeds
    removed and sliced
salt and pepper
1 tbsp finely chopped fresh
    cilantro
1 tbsp finely chopped
    fresh mint
1 tbsp finely chopped fresh
    parsley
several fresh basil leaves, torn

method

1 To shape noodle baskets, you will need a special set of 2 long-handled wire baskets that clip inside each other, available from gourmet kitchen stores. Dip the larger wire basket in oil, then line it completely and evenly with one-fourth of the tangled noodles. Dip the smaller wire basket in oil, then position it inside the larger basket and clip it into position.

2 Heat 4 inches/10 cm of oil in a wok or deep-fat fryer to 350–375°F/180–190°C, or until a cube of bread browns in 30 seconds. Lower the baskets into the oil and deep-fry for 2–3 minutes, or until the noodles are golden brown. Remove the baskets from the oil and drain on paper towels. Unclip the 2 wire baskets and carefully remove the small one. Use a round-bladed knife, if necessary, to prise the noodle basket from the wire frame. Repeat to make 3 more baskets. Let the noodle baskets cool.

3 To make the salad, combine the sour cream, mayonnaise, gingerroot, and lime rind. Gradually add the lime juice until you get the flavor you like. Stir in the chicken, carrot, cucumber, and seasoning to taste. Cover and let chill. Just before serving, stir in the herbs and spoon the salad into the noodle baskets.

teriyaki chicken with sesame noodles

ingredients

SERVES 4

4 boneless chicken breasts,
about 6 oz/175 g each,
with or without skin, as
you wish

about 4 tbsp bottled teriyaki
sauce, or homemade
teriyaki sauce

peanut or corn oil

cucumber fans, to garnish

sesame noodles

9 oz/250 g dried thin
buckwheat noodles

1 tbsp toasted sesame oil

2 tbsp toasted sesame seeds

2 tbsp finely chopped fresh
parsley

salt and pepper

method

1 Using a sharp knife, score each chicken breast diagonally across 3 times and rub all over with teriyaki sauce. Set aside to marinate for at least 10 minutes, or cover and let chill all day.

2 When you are ready to cook the chicken, preheat the broiler to high. Bring a pan of water to a boil, add the buckwheat noodles, and boil for 3 minutes, until soft. Alternatively, cook according to the package instructions. Drain and rinse well in cold water to stop the cooking and remove excess starch, then drain again.

3 Lightly brush the broiler rack with oil. Add the chicken breasts, skin-side up, and brush again with a little extra teriyaki sauce. Broil the chicken breasts about 4 inches/10 cm from the heat, brushing occasionally with extra teriyaki sauce, for 15 minutes, or until cooked through and the juices run clear.

4 Meanwhile, heat a wok over high heat. Add the sesame oil and heat until it shimmers. Add the noodles and stir round to heat through, then stir in the sesame seeds and parsley. Finally, add salt and pepper to taste.

5 Transfer the chicken breasts to plates and add a portion of noodles to each.

yaki soba

ingredients

SERVES 2

14 oz/400 g ramen noodles

1 onion, finely sliced

7 oz/200 g/1^1/$_3$ cups
    bean sprouts

1 red bell pepper, seeded and
    finely shredded

1 boneless, skin-on cooked
    chicken breast, about
    5^1/$_2$ oz/150 g, cooked
    and sliced

12 cooked shelled shrimp

1 tbsp oil

2 tbsp shoyu (Japanese
    soy sauce)

^{1}/$_2$ tbsp mirin

1 tsp sesame oil

1 tsp roasted sesame seeds

2 scallions, finely sliced

method

1 Cook the noodles according to the package instructions, drain well, and tip into a bowl.

2 Mix the onion, bean sprouts, red bell pepper, chicken, and shrimp together in a separate bowl. Stir through the noodles.

3 Preheat a wok over high heat. Add the oil and heat until very hot. Add the noodle mixture and stir-fry for 4 minutes, or until golden, then add the shoyu, mirin, and sesame oil and toss together.

4 Divide the mixture between 2 plates, sprinkle with the sesame seeds and scallions, and serve at once.

singapore noodles

ingredients

SERVES 4–6

10 1/2 oz/300 g thin rice
vermicelli

3 tbsp vegetable or peanut oil

2 garlic cloves, finely chopped

1 lb 2 oz/500 g small raw
shrimp, peeled, deveined
and chopped into
2–3 pieces

4 oz/115 g cha siu, julienned

1 onion, finely sliced

1 tbsp mild curry powder,
such as garam masala

1 green bell pepper, finely
sliced

1 tsp sugar

1 tsp salt

1–2 tsp chicken stock

1 tbsp light soy sauce

7 oz/200 g/1 1/3 cups bean
sprouts, trimmed

method

1 Cook the rice vermicelli according to
the directions on the package. Drain and
set aside.

2 In a preheated wok, heat 2 tablespoons
of the oil. Toss in the garlic and stir-fry until
fragrant. Add the shrimp and stir-fry for
1 minute, or until the shrimp are beginning to
change color. Add the cha siu and stir-fry for
1 more minute. Remove everything from the
wok and set aside.

3 In the clean wok, heat the remaining oil. Add
the onion and stir-fry for 1 minute, then stir in
the curry powder. Add the bell pepper, sugar,
salt, and stock and stir-fry for 2 minutes.
Pour in the light soy sauce followed by the
vermicelli. Toss well. Finally, add the bean
sprouts and the shrimp–pork mixture. Stir
until warmed through, then serve at once.

fish curry with rice noodles

ingredients

SERVES 4

2 tbsp vegetable or peanut oil

1 large onion, chopped

2 garlic cloves, chopped

3 oz/75 g white mushrooms

8 oz/225 g monkfish, cut into
cubes, each about 1 inch

8 oz/225 g salmon fillets, cut
into cubes, each about
1 inch

8 oz/225 g cod, cut into
cubes, each about 1 inch

2 tbsp Thai red curry paste

14 oz/400 g/1^3/$_4$ cups canned
coconut milk

handful of fresh cilantro,
chopped

1 tsp jaggery or soft light
brown sugar

1 tsp fish sauce

4 oz/115 g rice noodles

3 scallions, chopped

2 oz/50 g/^{1}/$_2$ cup bean
sprouts

few Thai basil leaves

method

1 Heat the oil in a wok and gently sauté the onion, garlic, and mushrooms until softened but not browned.

2 Add the fish, curry paste, and coconut milk and bring gently to a boil. Let simmer for 2–3 minutes before adding half the cilantro, the sugar, and fish sauce. Keep warm.

3 Meanwhile, soak the noodles for 3–4 minutes (check the package instructions) or until tender, and drain well through a colander. Put the colander and noodles over a pan of simmering water. Add the scallions, bean sprouts, and most of the basil and steam on top of the noodles for 1–2 minutes or until just wilted.

4 Pile the noodles onto warmed serving plates and top with the fish curry. Sprinkle the remaining cilantro and basil over the top and serve immediately.

stir-fried noodles with marinated fish

ingredients

SERVES 4

1 lb/450 g monkfish or cod,
  cubed

8 oz/225 g salmon fillets,
  cubed

2 tbsp vegetable or peanut oil

2 fresh green chiles, seeded
  and chopped

grated rind and juice of 1 lime

1 tbsp fish sauce

4 oz/115 g wide rice noodles

2 tbsp vegetable or peanut oil

2 shallots, sliced

2 garlic cloves, chopped
  finely

1 fresh red chile,
  seeded and chopped

2 tbsp Thai soy sauce

2 tbsp chili sauce

method

1 Place the fish in a shallow bowl. To make the marinade, mix the oil, green chiles, lime juice and rind, and fish sauce together and pour over the fish. Cover and chill for 2 hours.

2 Put the noodles in a bowl and cover with boiling water. Leave for 8–10 minutes (check the package instructions) and drain well.

3 Heat the oil in a wok and sauté the shallots, garlic, and red chile until lightly browned. Add the soy sauce and chili sauce. Add the fish and the marinade to the wok and stir-fry gently for 2–3 minutes until cooked through.

4 Add the drained noodles and stir gently. Sprinkle with cilantro and serve immediately.

curried noodles with shrimp & straw mushrooms

ingredients

SERVES 4

1 tbsp vegetable or peanut oil

3 shallots, chopped

1 fresh red chile, seeded and chopped

1 tbsp Thai red curry paste

1 lemongrass stalk (white part only), chopped finely

8 oz/225 g cooked shelled shrimp

14 oz/400 g canned straw mushrooms, drained

2 tbsp fish sauce

2 tbsp Thai soy sauce

8 oz/225 g fresh egg noodles

fresh cilantro, chopped, to garnish

method

1 Heat the oil in a wok and stir-fry the shallots and chile for 2–3 minutes. Add the curry paste and lemongrass and stir-fry for 2–3 minutes.

2 Add the shrimp, mushrooms, fish sauce, and soy sauce, and stir well to mix.

3 Meanwhile, cook the noodles in boiling water for 3–4 minutes, drain, and transfer to warmed plates. Top with the shrimp curry, sprinkle the cilantro over, and serve immediately.

spicy noodles with mushroom egg rolls

ingredients

SERVES 4

2 tbsp vegetable or peanut oil

1 small onion, chopped finely

8 oz/225 g mushrooms, chopped

1 tbsp Thai red curry paste

1 tbsp Thai soy sauce

1 tbsp fish sauce

8 square egg roll skins

vegetable or peanut oil, for deep-frying

8 oz/225 g quick-cook noodles

1 garlic clove, chopped

6 scallions, chopped

1 red bell pepper, seeded and chopped

1 tbsp ground coriander

1 tbsp ground cumin

method

1 Heat 1 tablespoon of the oil in a wok and stir-fry the onion and mushrooms until crisp and browned. Add the curry paste, soy sauce, and fish sauce, and stir-fry for 2–3 minutes. Remove the wok from the heat.

2 Spoon an eighth of the mixture across one of the egg roll skins and roll up, folding the sides over the filling to enclose it.

3 Heat the oil for deep-frying in a wok and deep-fry the egg rolls, 4 at a time, until crisp and browned. Drain on paper towels and keep warm.

4 Meanwhile, put the noodles in a bowl, cover with boiling water, and let swell.

5 Heat the remaining oil in the wok and stir-fry the garlic, scallions, and red bell pepper for 2–3 minutes. Stir in the coriander and cumin, then drain the noodles and add them to the wok. Toss together and serve topped with the egg rolls.

vegetarian

The cuisine of East and Southeast Asia, with its wonderful array of fresh vegetables, is perfectly suited to the vegetarian diet and wok cookery is the ideal way to ensure that the important nutrients are retained.

There is no dairy produce in this region, so cheese, a typical source of protein used in a vegetarian diet, is absent from these recipes. Instead, the protein is provided by nuts—try some delicious, vibrantly colored vegetables with roasted cashew nuts, made special by the addition of a sweet-and-sour sauce—and by bean curd. This is a curious but exceptionally nutritious food made from soy beans in a similar way to cheese. It usually comes in a slab, which can be cut into cubes, and has a completely bland taste that readily takes on flavor, making it ideal to use in curries and stir-fries. Try spicy bean curd—the curd will soak up the chile, garlic, and ginger flavors and if you've never tried it before, you will be converted!

These recipes also make excellent side dishes to accompany Asian dishes. Try some of the simple stir-fried vegetables as an accompaniment to rich meat dishes—for example, the stir-fried bean sprouts, Chinese greens, and long beans with red bell pepper would make an attractive selection. Good health!

eggplant with miso

ingredients

SERVES 4

2 eggplants

oil, for stir-frying

1 fresh red chile, sliced

2 tbsp sake

4 tbsp mirin

2 tbsp shoyu (Japanese
   soy sauce)

3 tbsp hatcho miso

2 tbsp water

method

1 Cut the eggplants into wedges.

2 Preheat a wok over high heat. Add a little oil and heat until very hot. Stir-fry the eggplant, in batches, for 4 minutes, or until browned and cooked through.

3 Return all the eggplant to the wok together with the chile and stir together. Add the remaining ingredients and toss everything together. Cook, stirring, until the sauce thickens. Serve immediately.

eggplant with red bell peppers

ingredients

SERVES 4

3 tbsp vegetable or peanut oil

1 garlic clove, finely chopped

3 eggplants, halved lengthwise
and cut diagonally into
1-inch/2.5-cm pieces

1 tsp white rice vinegar

1 red bell pepper, finely sliced

2 tbsp light soy sauce

1 tsp sugar

1 tbsp finely chopped cilantro
leaves (optional), to garnish

method

1 In a preheated wok, heat the oil. When it begins to smoke, toss in the garlic and stir-fry until fragrant, then add the eggplant pieces. Stir-fry for 30 seconds, then add the vinegar. Turn down the heat and cook, covered, for 5 minutes, stirring occasionally.

2 When the eggplant pieces are soft, add the bell pepper and stir. Add the light soy sauce and sugar and cook, uncovered, for 2 minutes.

3 Turn off the heat and let it rest for 2 minutes. Transfer to a dish, then garnish with chopped cilantro and serve.

mixed vegetables with quick-fried basil

ingredients

SERVES 4

2 tbsp vegetable or peanut oil

2 garlic cloves, chopped

1 onion, sliced

4 oz/115 g baby corn, cut in half diagonally

1/2 cucumber, peeled, halved, seeded, and sliced

8 oz/225 g canned water chestnuts, drained and rinsed

2 oz/55 g snow peas, trimmed

4 oz/115 g shiitake mushrooms, halved

1 red bell pepper, seeded and sliced thinly

1 tbsp jaggery or soft light brown sugar

2 tbsp Thai soy sauce

1 tbsp fish sauce

1 tbsp rice vinegar

boiled rice, to serve

quick-fried basil

vegetable or peanut oil, for cooking

8–12 sprigs fresh Thai basil

method

1 Heat the oil in a wok and stir-fry the garlic and onion for 1–2 minutes. Add the corn, cucumber, water chestnuts, snow peas, mushrooms, and red bell pepper, and stir-fry for 2–3 minutes, until starting to soften.

2 Add the sugar, soy sauce, fish sauce, and vinegar, and gradually bring to a boil. Let simmer for 1–2 minutes.

3 Meanwhile, heat the oil for the basil in a wok and, when hot, add the basil sprigs. Cook for 20–30 seconds, until crisp. Remove with a slotted spoon and drain on paper towels.

4 Garnish the vegetable stir-fry with the crispy basil and serve immediately, with the boiled rice.

sweet-&-sour vegetables with cashews

ingredients

SERVES 4

1 tbsp vegetable or peanut oil

1 tsp chili oil

2 onions, sliced

2 carrots, sliced thinly

2 zucchinis, sliced thinly

4 oz/115 g head broccoli, cut
into florets

4 oz/115 g/2$^{1}/_{4}$ cups white
mushrooms, sliced

4 oz/115 g small bok choy,
halved

2 tbsp jaggery or soft light
brown sugar

2 tbsp Thai soy sauce

1 tbsp rice vinegar

2 oz/55 g/scant $^{1}/_{2}$ cup
cashews

method

1 Heat the vegetable or peanut oil and the chili oil in a wok and stir-fry the onions for 1–2 minutes, until they start to soften.

2 Add the carrots, zucchinis, and broccoli, and stir-fry for 2–3 minutes. Add the mushrooms, bok choy, sugar, soy sauce, and rice vinegar, and stir-fry for 1–2 minutes.

3 Meanwhile, dry-fry or toast the cashews. Sprinkle the cashews over the stir-fry and serve immediately.

hot-&-sour cabbage

ingredients

SERVES 4

1 lb/450 g firm white cabbage

1 tbsp vegetable or peanut oil

10 Sichuan peppers or more,
   to taste

3 dried chiles, coarsely
   chopped

$1/2$ tsp salt

1 tsp white rice vinegar

dash of sesame oil

pinch of sugar

method

1 To prepare the cabbage, discard the outer leaves and tough stems. Chop the cabbage into 1$1/4$-inch/ 3-cm squares, breaking up the chunks. Rinse thoroughly in cold water.

2 In a preheated wok, heat the oil and cook the peppers until fragrant. Stir in the chiles. Throw in the cabbage, a little at a time, together with the salt, and stir-fry for 2 minutes.

3 Add the vinegar, sesame oil, and sugar and cook for an additional minute, or until the cabbage is tender. Serve immediately.

spicy green beans

ingredients

SERVES 4

7 oz/200 g/generous
   $1^1/_4$ cups green beans,
   trimmed and cut
   diagonally into 3–4 pieces
2 tbsp vegetable or peanut oil
4 dried chiles, cut into
   2 or 3 pieces
$^1/_2$ tsp Sichuan peppers
1 garlic clove, finely sliced
6 thin slices of fresh gingerroot
2 scallions, white part only, cut
   diagonally into thin pieces
pinch of sea salt

method

1 Blanch the beans in a large pan of boiling water for 30 seconds. Drain and set aside.

2 In a preheated wok, heat 1 tablespoon of the oil. Over low heat, stir-fry the beans for about 5 minutes, or until they are beginning to wrinkle. Remove and set aside.

3 Add the remaining oil and stir-fry the chiles and peppers until they are fragrant. Add the garlic, gingerroot, and scallions and stir-fry until they begin to soften. Throw in the beans and toss to mix, then add the sea salt and serve immediately.

cauliflower & beans with cashews

ingredients

SERVES 4

1 tbsp vegetable or peanut oil

1 tbsp chili oil

1 onion, chopped

2 garlic cloves, chopped

2 tbsp Thai red curry paste

1 small cauliflower, cut into florets

6 oz/175 g yard-long beans, cut into 3-inch lengths

5 fl oz/150 ml/^{2}/$_3$ cup vegetable stock

2 tbsp Thai soy sauce

1^3/$_4$ oz/50 g/scant ^{1}/$_3$ cup toasted cashews, to garnish

method

1 Heat both the oils in a wok and stir-fry the onion and garlic until softened. Add the curry paste and stir-fry for 1–2 minutes.

2 Add the cauliflower and beans and stir-fry for 3–4 minutes, until softened. Pour in the stock and soy sauce and let simmer for 1–2 minutes. Serve immediately, garnished with the cashews.

julienne vegetable salad

ingredients

SERVES 4

4 tbsp vegetable or peanut oil

8 oz/225 g bean curd with herbs, cubed

1 red onion, sliced

4 scallions, cut into 2-inch lengths

1 garlic clove, chopped

2 carrots, cut into short, thin sticks

4 oz/115 g fine green beans, trimmed

1 yellow bell pepper, seeded and cut into strips

4 oz/115 g broccoli, cut into florets

1 large zucchini, cut into short, thin sticks

2 oz/55 g/$\frac{1}{2}$ cup bean sprouts

2 tbsp Thai red curry paste

4 tbsp Thai soy sauce

1 tbsp rice wine vinegar

1 tsp jaggery or soft light brown sugar

few Thai basil leaves

12 oz/350 g rice vermicelli noodles

method

1 Heat the oil in a wok and cook the bean curd cubes for 3–4 minutes, until browned on all sides. Lift the cubes out of the oil and drain on paper towels.

2 Add the onions, scallions, garlic, and carrots to the hot oil and cook for 1–2 minutes before adding the rest of the vegetables, except for the bean sprouts. Stir-fry for 2–3 minutes. Add the bean sprouts, then stir in the curry paste, soy, vinegar, sugar, and basil leaves. Cook for 30 seconds.

3 Soak the noodles in boiling water or stock for 2–3 minutes (check the package instructions) or until tender, and drain well.

4 Pile the vegetables onto the noodles, and serve topped with the bean curd cubes. Garnish with extra basil if desired.

oyster mushrooms & vegetables with peanut chili sauce

ingredients

SERVES 4

1 tbsp sesame oil

4 scallions, sliced finely

1 carrot, cut into batons

1 zucchini, cut into batons

1/2 head of broccoli,
    cut into florets

1 lb/450 g/9 cups oyster
    mushrooms,
    sliced thinly

2 tbsp coarse peanut butter

1 tsp chili powder, or to taste

3 tbsp water

wedges of lime, to garnish

cooked rice or noodles,
    to serve

method

1 Heat the oil in a wok until almost smoking. Stir-fry the scallions for 1 minute. Add the carrot and zucchini and stir-fry for another minute. Then add the broccoli and cook for one more minute.

2 Stir in the mushrooms and cook until they are soft and at least half the liquid they produce has evaporated. Add the peanut butter and stir well. Season with the chili powder to taste. Finally, add the water and cook for one more minute.

3 Serve over rice or noodles and garnish with wedges of lime.

broccoli & snow pea stir-fry

ingredients

SERVES 4

2 tbsp vegetable or peanut oil

dash of sesame oil

1 garlic clove, finely chopped

8 oz/225 g small broccoli florets

4 oz/115 g/1 cup snow peas,
    trimmed

8 oz/225 g Chinese cabbage,
    chopped into $1/2$-inch/
    1-cm slices

5–6 scallions, finely chopped

$1/2$ tsp salt

2 tbsp light soy sauce

1 tbsp Shaoxing rice wine

1 tsp sesame seeds, lightly
    toasted

method

1 In a preheated wok, heat the oils, then add the garlic and stir-fry vigorously. Add all the vegetables and salt and stir-fry over high heat, tossing rapidly, for about 3 minutes.

2 Pour in the light soy sauce and Shaoxing and cook for an additional 2 minutes. Sprinkle with the sesame seeds and serve hot.

stir-fried long beans with red bell pepper

ingredients

SERVES 4–6

10 oz/280 g long beans, cut
    into 2^1/$_2$-inch/6-cm lengths
1 tbsp vegetable or peanut oil
1 red bell pepper, slivered
pinch of salt
pinch of sugar

method

1 Blanch the beans in a large pan of boiling water for 30 seconds. Drain and set aside.

2 In a preheated wok, heat the oil and stir-fry the beans for 1 minute over high heat. Add the pepper and stir-fry for 1 more minute. Sprinkle the salt and sugar on top and serve.

spicy vegetarian stir-fry

ingredients

SERVES 4

3 tbsp vegetable oil

$1/2$ tsp turmeric

8 oz/225 g potatoes, cut into
  $1/2$ inch/1 cm cubes

3 shallots, chopped finely

1 bay leaf

$1/2$ tsp ground cumin

1 tsp finely grated fresh
  gingerroot

$1/4$ tsp chili powder

4 tomatoes, chopped coarsely

$10^1/2$ oz/300 g spinach
  (de-stalked), chopped
  coarsely

$4^1/2$ oz/125 g/$1^1/4$ cups fresh
  or frozen peas

1 tbsp lemon juice

salt and pepper

cooked basmati rice, to serve

method

1 In a wok, heat 2 tablespoons of the oil and add the turmeric and a pinch of salt. Carefully add the potatoes, stirring continuously to coat in the turmeric. Stir-fry for 5 minutes, then remove from the wok and set aside.

2 Heat the remaining tablespoon of oil and stir-fry the shallots for 1–2 minutes. Mix in the bay leaf, cumin, gingerroot, and chili powder, then add the tomatoes and stir-fry for 2 minutes.

3 Add the spinach, mixing well to combine all the flavors. Cover and simmer for 2–3 minutes. Return the potatoes to the wok and add the peas and lemon juice. Cook for 5 minutes, or until the potatoes are tender.

4 Remove the wok from the heat and discard the bay leaf, then season with salt and pepper. Serve with cooked basmati rice.

stir-fried chinese greens

ingredients

SERVES 4

1 tbsp vegetable or peanut oil

1 tsp finely chopped garlic

8 oz/225 g leafy Chinese
greens, coarsely chopped

$^1/_2$ tsp salt

method

1 In a preheated wok, heat the oil and stir-fry the garlic until fragrant. Over high heat, toss in the Chinese greens and salt and stir-fry for 1 minute maximum. Serve immediately.

stir-fried beansprouts

ingredients

SERVES 4

1 tbsp vegetable or peanut oil

8 oz/225 g/generous
1^1/$_2$ cups bean
sprouts, trimmed

2 tbsp finely chopped scallion

^{1}/$_2$ tsp salt

pinch of sugar

method

1 In a preheated wok, heat the oil and stir-fry the bean sprouts with the scallion for about 1 minute. Add the salt and sugar and stir.

2 Remove and serve immediately.

eggplant & bean curry

ingredients

SERVES 4

2 tbsp vegetable or peanut oil

1 onion, chopped

2 garlic cloves, crushed

2 fresh red chiles, seeded
and chopped

1 tbsp Thai red curry paste

1 large eggplant, cut into
chunks

4 oz/115 g pea or small
eggplants

4 oz/115 g/generous 1 cup
baby fava beans

4 oz/115 g fine green beans

10 fl oz/300 ml/1^{1}/$_{4}$ cups
vegetable stock

2 oz/55 g block creamed
coconut, chopped

3 tbsp Thai soy sauce

1 tsp jaggery or soft light
brown sugar

3 kaffir lime leaves, torn
coarsely

4 tbsp chopped fresh cilantro

method

1 Heat the oil in a wok and sauté the onion, garlic, and chiles for 1–2 minutes. Stir in the curry paste and cook for 1–2 minutes.

2 Add the eggplants and cook for 3–4 minutes, until starting to soften. (You may need to add a little more oil as eggplants soak it up quickly.) Add all the beans and stir-fry for 2 minutes.

3 Pour in the stock and add the creamed coconut, soy sauce, sugar, and lime leaves. Bring gently to a boil and cook until the coconut has dissolved. Stir in the cilantro and serve hot.

onion, potato & red bell pepper curry

ingredients

SERVES 4

2 tbsp vegetable or peanut oil

2 red onions, sliced

2 garlic cloves, chopped finely

2-inch piece fresh gingerroot, chopped finely

1 fresh red chile, seeded and chopped

1 tbsp Thai red curry paste

8 oz/225 g potatoes, cut into cubes, boiled for 5 minutes, and drained

2 red bell peppers, seeded and diced

10 fl oz/300 ml/1$\frac{1}{4}$ cups vegetable stock

1 tsp salt

4 tbsp chopped fresh cilantro

method

1 Heat the oil in a wok and stir-fry the onions, garlic, gingerroot, and chile for 2–3 minutes. Add the curry paste and stir-fry over low heat for 2–3 minutes.

2 Add the potatoes, bell peppers, stock, and salt, and cook for 3–4 minutes, until all the vegetables are tender. Stir in the cilantro and serve immediately.

zucchini & cashew nut curry

ingredients

SERVES 4

2 tbsp vegetable or peanut oil

6 scallions, chopped

2 garlic cloves, chopped

2 fresh green chiles, seeded and chopped

1 lb/450 g zucchinis, cut into thick slices

4 oz/115 g shiitake mushrooms, halved

2 oz/50 g/$1/2$ cup bean sprouts

3 oz/75 g/$1/2$ cup cashews, toasted or dry-fried

few Chinese chives, chopped

4 tbsp Thai soy sauce

1 tsp fish sauce

rice or noodles, to serve

method

1 Heat the oil in a wok and sauté the scallions, garlic, and chiles for 1–2 minutes, until softened but not browned.

2 Add the zucchinis and mushrooms and cook for 2–3 minutes until tender.

3 Add the bean sprouts, nuts, chives, and both sauces and stir-fry for 1–2 minutes.

4 Serve hot with rice or noodles.

bean curd & green vegetable curry

ingredients

SERVES 4

vegetable or peanut oil,
  for deep-frying
8 oz/225 g firm bean curd,
  cut into cubes
2 tbsp vegetable or peanut oil
1 tbsp chili oil
2 fresh green chiles, seeded
  and sliced
2 garlic cloves, crushed
6 scallions, sliced
2 medium zucchinis,
  cut into sticks
^{1}/2 cucumber, peeled,
  seeded, and sliced
1 green bell pepper, seeded
  and sliced
1 small head broccoli, cut
  into florets
2 oz/55 g fine green beans,
  halved
2 oz/55 g scant ^{1}/2 cup
  frozen peas, thawed
10 fl oz/300 ml/1^1/4 cups
  vegetable stock
2 oz/55 g block creamed
  coconut, chopped
2 tbsp Thai soy sauce
1 tsp soft light brown sugar
4 tbsp chopped fresh parsley,
  to garnish

method

1 Heat the oil for deep-frying in a wok and carefully lower in the bean curd cubes, in batches, and cook for 2–3 minutes, until golden brown. Remove with a slotted spoon and drain on paper towels.

2 Heat the other oils in a wok and stir-fry the chiles, garlic, and scallions for 2–3 minutes. Add the zucchinis, cucumber, green bell pepper, broccoli, and green beans, and stir-fry for an additional 2–3 minutes.

3 Add the peas, stock, coconut, soy sauce, and sugar. Cover and let simmer for 2–3 minutes, until all the vegetables are tender and the coconut has dissolved.

4 Stir in the bean curd and serve immediately, sprinkled with the parsley.

agedashi dofu

ingredients

SERVES 2

5 fl oz/150 ml/²/₃ cup water

2 tsp dashi granules

2 tbsp shoyu (Japanese
    soy sauce)

2 tbsp mirin

vegetable oil, for deep-frying

10¹/₂ oz/300 g silken bean
    curd, drained on paper
    towels and cut into
    4 cubes

2 tbsp all-purpose flour

1 tsp grated fresh gingerroot

2 tsp grated daikon

¹/₄ tsp kezuri-bushi shavings

method

1 Put the water in a pan with the dashi granules and bring to a boil. Add the shoyu and mirin and cook for 1 minute. Keep warm.

2 Preheat a wok, then fill one-third full with oil, or use a deep-fryer. Heat the oil to 350–375°F/180–190°C, or until a cube of bread browns in 30 seconds. Meanwhile, dust the bean curd cubes with the flour.

3 Add the bean curd to the oil, in batches, and cook until lightly golden in color. Remove, drain on paper towels, and keep hot while you cook the remaining bean curd cubes.

4 Put 2 pieces of bean curd in each of 2 bowls and divide the dashi stock between them. Top with gingerroot, daikon, and kezuri-bushi.

vegetables with bean curd & spinach

ingredients

SERVES 4

vegetable or peanut oil, for
    deep-frying
8 oz/225 g firm bean curd,
    drained and cut into
    cubes
2 tbsp vegetable or peanut oil
2 onions, chopped
2 garlic cloves, chopped
1 fresh red chile, seeded
    and sliced
3 celery stalks, sliced
    diagonally
8 oz/225 g/4^1/$_2$ cups
    mushrooms, sliced thickly
4 oz/115 g baby corn,
    cut in half
1 red bell pepper, seeded and
    cut into strips
3 tbsp Thai red curry paste
14 fl oz/400 g/1^3/$_4$ cups
    coconut milk
1 tsp jaggery or soft light
    brown sugar
2 tbsp Thai soy sauce
8 oz/225 g/5 cups baby
    spinach leaves

method

1 Heat the oil in a wok and deep-fry the bean curd cubes, in batches, for 4–5 minutes, until crisp and browned. Remove with a slotted spoon and drain on paper towels.

2 Heat 2 tablespoons of the oil in a wok and stir-fry the onions, garlic, and chile for 1–2 minutes, until they start to soften. Add the celery, mushrooms, corn, and red bell pepper, and stir-fry for 3–4 minutes, until they soften.

3 Stir in the curry paste and coconut milk and gradually bring to a boil. Add the sugar and soy sauce and then the spinach. Cook, stirring constantly, until the spinach has wilted. Serve immediately, topped with the bean curd.

bamboo shoots with bean curd

ingredients

SERVES 4–6

3 dried Chinese mushrooms,
   soaked in warm water
   for 20 minutes

2 oz/55 g baby bok choy

vegetable or peanut oil,
   for deep-frying

1 lb/450 g firm bean curd,
   cut into 1-inch/2.5-cm
   squares

4 oz/115 g/^{1}/$_2$ cup fresh or
   canned bamboo shoots,
   rinsed and finely sliced (if
   using fresh shoots, boil in
   water first for 30 minutes)

1 tsp oyster sauce

1 tsp light soy sauce

method

1 Squeeze out any excess water from the mushrooms and finely slice, discarding any tough stems. Blanch the bok choy in a large pan of boiling water for 30 seconds. Drain and set aside.

2 Heat enough oil for deep-frying in a wok or deep-fat fryer until it reaches 350–375°F/ 180–190°C, or until a cube of bread browns in 30 seconds. Cook the bean curd cubes until golden brown. Remove, then drain and set aside.

3 In a preheated wok, heat 1 tablespoon of the oil, then toss in the mushrooms and bok choy and stir. Add the bean curd and bamboo shoots with the oyster and soy sauces. Heat through and serve.

spicy bean curd

ingredients

SERVES 4

marinade

2¹/₂ fl oz/75 ml/¹/₃ cup
vegetable bouillon

2 tsp cornstarch

2 tbsp soy sauce

1 tbsp superfine sugar

pinch of chile flakes

stir-fry

9 oz/250 g firm bean curd,
rinsed and drained
thoroughly and cut into
¹/₂ inch/1 cm cubes

4 tbsp peanut oil

1 tbsp grated fresh gingerroot

3 garlic cloves, crushed

4 scallions, sliced thinly

1 head of broccoli, cut
into florets

1 carrot, cut into batons

1 yellow bell pepper, sliced
thinly

9 oz/250 g/5 cups shiitake
mushrooms,
sliced thinly

steamed rice, to serve

method

1 Blend the vegetable bouillon, cornstarch, soy sauce, sugar, and chile flakes together in a large bowl. Add the bean curd and toss well to coat. Set aside to marinate for 20 minutes.

2 In a wok, heat 2 tablespoons of the peanut oil and stir-fry the bean curd with its marinade until brown and crispy. Remove from the wok and set aside.

3 Heat the remaining 2 tablespoons of peanut oil in the wok and stir-fry the gingerroot, garlic, and scallions for 30 seconds. Add the broccoli, carrot, yellow bell pepper, and mushrooms to the wok and cook for 5–6 minutes. Return the bean curd to the wok and stir-fry to reheat. Serve immediately over steamed rice.